THE

HACIENDA

IN

MEXICO

DANIEL NIERMAN AND
ERNESTO H. VALLEJO

■

MARDITH SCHUETZ-MILLER,
TRANSLATOR

FOREWORD BY
ELENA PONIATOWSKA

THE HACIENDA IN MEXICO

UNIVERSITY OF TEXAS PRESS
AUSTIN

FRONTISPIECE:
Ciénega de Mata. View of the compound.

ROGER FULLINGTON

SERIES IN

ARCHITECTURE

Publication of this book was made possible
in part by support from Roger Fullington,
the SBC Foundation, and a challenge grant from
the National Endowment for the Humanities.

∞ The paper used in this book meets the minimum
requirements of ANSI/NISO Z39.48-992 (R1997)
(Permanence of Paper).

LIBRARY OF CONGRESS CATALOGING-IN-PUBLICATION DATA

Nierman, Daniel.
[La hacienda en México. English]
The hacienda in Mexico / by Daniel Nierman and
Ernesto H. Vallejo ; translated by Mardith Schuetz-Miller ;
foreword by Elena Poniatowska.—1st ed.
p.   cm.
Includes bibliographical references.
ISBN 0-292-70526-3 (alk. paper)
1. Haciendas—Mexico.   2. Farm buildings—Mexico.
I. Vallejo, Ernesto H.   II. Title.
NA8206.M6   N5413   2003
728'.6' 0972—dc21   2002152503

———

To our parents,

whose support

and encouragement

were an inspiration

———

CONTENTS

LIST OF
ILLUSTRATED HACIENDAS

A SINGLE GLANCE is sufficient to see that Daniel Nierman and Ernesto Vallejo are true artists; with a second look, one is moved by the meticulously drafted plans, the repeating arcades, the mass of the walls, and the grandeur of the proportions. Daniel Nierman and Ernesto Vallejo rescue from oblivion those eye-opening jewels that are the haciendas of the sixteenth to the twentieth century that God (a Spanish God, naturally) seems to have cast from his cloud onto the extensive voids of Mexico, which, with the sudden apparition of Zontecomate,[1] make us rub our eyes in order to assure us that this is no illusion.

To the astonishment of the traveler who proceeds from barren plot to barren plot in the desert, enveloped in a halo of dust, there suddenly appears a hacienda such as Espejel, with its aureola of pure gold and its fairytale balustrades and cornices. "Is this real or am I dreaming?" The pulque-producing hacienda, with its *tinacal* and press, also has a billiard table for the enjoyment of the owner and his guests, beveled mirrors that reflect the throats and silk lace of the décolleté, the red or black wavy hair of women who look like Carlotta, bucolic murals painted in the style of Watteau, nymphs holding pitchers arranged around the fountain, gardens recalling Versailles, and the chapel—the only place in which both owners and servants come together. Bless me if this isn't what servants' stairs are for, as well as the back door, the field gate for the use of the Indians, the copper-colored race, the day laborers, and the resident peons, who, after chapel, have access only to the office of the administrator where he gives them their orders.

Daniel Nierman and Ernesto Vallejo traversed Mexico to find the haciendas that concern us here: Mala Yerba and Mal País, San Miguel Regla and Santa Agueda, Tenejac and San Miguel Tesmelucan, Pozo del Carmen and Ciénega de Mata, San Diego and Santiago, Jaral de Berrio and La Ventilla, Tecajete, Peotillos, Tepetates, Peñasco, and Bledos, measuring the property and showing the relationship of its buildings and fields, the circumference of the cisterns, water troughs, beds as big as boats, and armoires with crownwork that might have fitted the emperor Maximilian better than his pine box. On their architectural tablets they drew, one by one, the habitations with their washstands and porcelain jars, the chests and stools that lined the interior patio, the one with the pots of geraniums and ferns. By recording the plans of each granary, each storeroom, by siting corrals and confessionals, Daniel Nierman and Ernesto Vallejo became custodians—better yet, guardians—of this ritual of jasmines and orange trees, mesquites, nopal cacti, magueys, and *pirules* that constitutes the hacienda. As officiants, they became protagonists of the Mass and put themselves at the service of this ancient rite of the haciendas, which in the mid–sixteenth century were called "forms for taking away labor and bread." The result of the foregoing, coupled with their sublime surveys and ink drawings (on *albanene* paper, which has a consistency like that of the Host), is this magic book, *The Hacienda in Mexico*. Through the delicacy of their drawings, which seem to be embroidered by a diligent ant, we see every one of the rounded stones in the pavement, each bay in the naves, each flight of steps leading to the altar, the purity of the lines, the unequaled strength of the buttresses,

and the baroque richness of the altar, over whose volutes and curves pose shafts of light, exposing them, polishing them just as the air and wind, water and time burnish the walls, the roof, and the great doors, giving them their color and texture. They considered everything: natural phenomena, the stuccoed border of the ceiling, and in the rooms that want to be seen as European, carved wooden rocking chairs with neoclassic devices sculpted on them, the unreachable rafters like rails lining the ceiling. The result is that the dining room is always the grandest in the hacienda, and the kitchens are high, wide, and big—opening onto a terrace bleached by the sun, large and wise like a good cook who tastes with spoon in hand, plucks feathers, washes, hangs clothes in the sun, mixes dough, makes tortillas, air-dries and smokes food, cools water, grinds, and preserves. All of the above requires these high ceilings toward which climb numerous jars and crocks, large kitchen ranges, door and window recesses lined with flower pots and Mobil Oil cans planted with sweet basil, marjoram, chamomile, and chives grown by the cook, who cuts epazote, cilantro, parsley, and mint as needed—miraculous species that manage to grow from the expanse of the earth, the same earth next to

the big house, the atrium of the chapel, and the ubiquitous wall that turns rocky and orange, a worn-out, primeval soil whose sediment is the essence of the hacienda itself.

The photographs, the large close-ups, appear to contain the mold and the very flavor of the stone. What a pity that one cannot see the colors that Daniel captured; they are unpublished colors that would have been envied by Tàpies and Tamayo,[2] purples and greens born before the creation of the world. Never in our country has an architectural study of the haciendas been made; never before was there a typological study of all the spaces. Now, with the work of Nierman and Vallejo, we are able to return to the daily life of the hacienda as it was: the equipment, the carriage, the daily awakening, the humid night, and the sleeplessness. José María Velasco, Luis Barragán, and Juan Rulfo[3] would feel themselves fortunate to thumb the pages of such a book, capable of capturing the essence of what they wanted to sow: the Mexico of the spirit and the fortitude to resist the onslaught of time, that of the land and the rock, the maize and the maguey, and the clay that sounds like silver, as López Velarde[4] used to say.

INTRODUCTION

THE HACIENDA, an institution intimately linked to our country's past, has been the subject of several studies. These works have approached the hacienda from different viewpoints: historical, economic, and political. However, the architecture of the hacienda has never been the focus of attention. It is for this reason that we, as architects and Mexicans, decided to undertake this investigation with the aim of opening another road toward awareness of our architecture.

From the vast range of Mexican haciendas we decided to work one geographic area, which we considered sufficient to establish the constants that one can assume, with a certain validity, are true of all the others. These similarities stand out even more among the many differences that we observed in the sample that was the object of our study. The haciendas we studied are located in the states of Hidalgo, Tlaxcala, and San Luis Potosí. They are representative of centers of agricultural and livestock production and were constructed and modified from the sixteenth until the beginning of the twentieth century.

To accomplish our task, we planned a course of action to familiarize ourselves with the world of the hacienda and to work out the basic concepts of this institution from an architectural point of view. We first undertook reconnaissance visits of haciendas that allowed us to observe and distinguish the different characteristics. Then we conducted a bibliographic survey that permitted us to identify and classify the information we obtained from this complex world. Once our data were interpreted, we created a register composed of photographs, written observations, and drawn elevations. To this point, the paths we followed were general. Nevertheless, the character of our work obliged us to try diverse procedures and to make use of the most varied sources of information—from the review of old plans to consultation of modern databases, from conversations with those in charge to interviews with the actual owners of the hacienda archives, from municipal functionaries to state and federal authorities.

To accomplish the first visits, we had to

travel more than 15,000 kilometers, because the information we had on any given location—plans, lists, historic accounts, catalogues—did not always correspond to present-day maps. In these sometimes unfruitful travels, however, we also came across some haciendas unknown to us. As we became more deeply engrossed in our study, we needed the approval and authorization of the proprietors more and more to take photographs and to make drawings and measurements.

The result of this work—expressed through the plans, photographs, and written infor-mation—sustained our initial goal: to discover the architectural constants in the world of the Mexican haciendas. Later, with a view that these results could be useful to others, we opted to present the data in this form.

Thus, our initial hypothesis, with which we presumed we would find architectural elements specific to Mexico, in an institution so singularly ours, was amply proved.

CHAPTER ONE

THE

HACIENDA

THROUGH

TIME

THE HACIENDA, an institution of agrarian exploitation, was one of the important pillars of Mexico's economic life from the colonial period until the Revolution and, along with *encomiendas* and mining, a fundamental element in Mexico's colonization. Their antecedents date to the medieval forms of production consolidated during the reconquest of southern Spain by means of *repartimientos* and *encomiendas*. These grants, given to the noblemen of northern Spain in return for their sustaining the armed forces and protecting the "Divine Cult," were still present in the memory of the conquerors of Mexico. "These forms of colonization found in the New World an appropriate context for their implantation that had its origins in diverse factors within the social and economic evolution of the Aztec Empire. The factors that logically paved the way for the Spaniards," Chevalier tells us, "pertained to the development of the livestock industry, agriculture, and the distribution of lands within the indigenous communities."[1]

Livestock raising in pre-Hispanic Mexico did not count as a means of production, since working animals were almost nonexistent. Agriculture had developed in the fertile and well-irrigated zones along the banks of rivers and lakes. Such limited occupation of the land left great empty spaces for the reproduction and grazing of the Spaniards' livestock. Prior to the arrival of the conquerors there already existed a marked tendency toward the establishment of territorial dominions in the hands of the *pillis*, or nobility, to the detriment of the clans, or *calpullis*. "This existence of individual ownership in Aztec society, as well as its tributary relationship with its governed territories, further facilitated the way for the Spaniards, who replaced the old masters in the receipt of tribute and substituted the new Spanish nobility in possession of the land."[2]

The reactivation of the economy in the recently conquered colony was based on precious metals, which provided true wealth and was also the only monetary exchange with Europe. The rich silver deposits of Mexico propelled a colonial expansion into unpopulated and arid areas, where these outposts were separated from each other and from the capital by thousands of kilometers. Moreover, in 1529, *cédulas* of concession appeared whereby the Spaniards had the right to receive tribute and the services of Indian labor. The *encomiendas* were of diverse magnitude: some comprised great expanses with thousands of tributaries, and others were only small villages lost in the mountains. Each establishment was not only a place consisting of a plaza, a church, and a cluster of houses, but also represented a moral body, a community of medieval traditions jealous of its autonomy and rights—an institution. Through the *encomiendas* was channeled a labor force necessary for the development of mining and agriculture.

The Spanish state, eager for resources, sought the most efficacious means of protecting the routes to the mining operations and did so in part by facilitating the establishment of small settlements devoted to agriculture and stock raising along the length of these routes.

La Noria. Tlaxcala.
Hacienda worker inside the
tinacal.

These settlements came to benefit from the demand for provisions and livestock required by the mining communities.

As early as 1523 the king recommended to Cortés that he award Spaniards of recently founded cities "their holdings of *caballerías* or *peonías*, according to the person's status."[3] Some Spaniards, however, not wanting to be judged of inferior rank, already considered themselves *caballeros* or *hidalgos*. The area of *caballerías* was "10 *fanegas* for sowing wheat, or 43 hectares," and *peonías* were five times smaller. Owing to the scarcity of vegetables, fruit, and cereals, principally wheat, of peninsular origin, since 1529 these farm grants were intended for the cultivation of this cereal under the terms of the *encomienda*—to the point that a cultivated

caballería and a wheat field were synonymous during the first half of the sixteenth century. The more remote cities granted titles of ownership without the confirmation of superior authorities, and as the landholders formed quickly into local oligarchies, land concessions expanded into haciendas in many cases. In the mid–sixteenth century, a name was coined to designate agricultural operations: "farms for taking away labor and bread." These arose from the labor services taken away from the *encomenderos* after 1549 and redistributed among Spaniards who cultivated wheat. "This system of *repartimiento* signaled a notable improvement for the Indians because they were no longer obliged to work by a master, but by representatives of the justice system, who did not have

Ocotepec. Main patio.

the same interest in Indian labor as the *encomenderos* and only proportioned the man-power that they considered would be bene-ficial to the 'Republic' of the Spaniards."[4]

During the epoch of heavy labor, judges in charge of labor distribution authorized Indian teams from villages near the farms to perform the work. A parallel work force was made up of free Indians who hired themselves out on their own initiative. These workers were detained by their masters for long periods of time on ac-count of not being able to repay the advances given them. Although this type of servitude per-tains more to the seventeenth century, and later to the nineteenth, at this time a new economic form typical of haciendas began to develop.

Early on, the Spaniards showed dissatisfaction with a single *caballería*. Sometimes, thanks to multiple grants, other times, through sale to fa-vored Spanish beneficiaries, to Indian caciques, or else by cornering unoccupied lands, they began to form properties of three, eight, fifteen, eighty-six *caballerías*, and even more. These estates were not dedicated solely to agricultural production. In many instances, they were combined with the raising of sheep or hogs, and the ranch was designated for "husbandry and livestock," and in addition to their *caballerías*, took in extensions for pasturage comprising one or several 780-hectare sites.

"*Estancias* were not occupied year-round by the owners; some Indians or Negroes lived on them, but not always the Spanish family. A 1569 statistic shows that only 200 Spaniards, out of the 8,000 who inhabited the capital, regularly lived on the 150 *estancias* owned by the archbishopric of Mexico."[5]

Discounting some very important ranches or some sugar plantations, grand constructions were reserved for urban residences, at least until the late seventeenth century. This explains why there are no traces of farm buildings. They were generally constructed of adobe, rarely of stone, and thatched with straw or shingled—in contrast to the grand sugar plantations, such as one belonging to Cortés, which in 1549 was already of impressive size. From early on, sugar plantations called for a new kind of farming operation in which the natives were integrated and conformed to a new type of social organization. These plantations were almost completely self-sufficient, and from the sixteenth century onward became the forerunners of the classic Mexican haciendas.

The predominant factor in the formation of the grand properties in Mexico was livestock raising, according to Chevalier. "The new continent offered favorable environments for the rapid increase of livestock. The existence of large open spaces was well established, since from the initial colonization of New Spain, the Castilian traditions of common grazing and transhumance were put into effect."[6]

The growth of the herds reached such magnitude that ranchers very quickly lost control over them. The principal consequence of this problem was the invasion of Indian agricultural fields by livestock, which the authorities showed a certain willingness to ignore for the sake of livestock increase.

About the sixteenth century a new term appeared in Mexico "that defined the limit of man and loose herds: the *estancia,* the etymology of which evokes very different concepts than transhumance and common grazing. The word *estancia* implies the birth of certain rights over places so designated. Its early sense was precise and denoted a site designated for livestock, as one sees in the acts of the cabildo of Mexico City between 1527 and 1530."[7]

"Spaniards interested in dedicating themselves to the breeding of livestock should appeal to the *ayuntamiento* to receive an acknowledgment of the determined 'site or seat.' The beneficiary would then have the right to prohibit any other livestock owner from establishing a new center for that purpose within one league roundabout for sheep or cows and a half league for hogs. Ranchers were prohibited from placing their establishments any closer than a half league from fields already cultivated by natives or farmers."[8]

Estancias were divided into two groups: those for cattle (large livestock) and those for sheep, goats, and hogs (small livestock). The areas fixed in about 1567 were 1,750 hectares for large livestock and 780 hectares for small livestock. Here the *estancia* took on its definitive form and was an important step toward the final makeup of haciendas. Since livestock raising was becoming, after mining, the principal economic resource of the country, it was advantageous to encourage it—above all in distant regions—by bestowing titles in the form of grazing. It is worth mentioning that such issues were not precarious concessions, but definite and transmissible rights guaranteed from this time forward by the direct representative of the king of Spain. *Estancias*, like *caballerías*, were subject to sale or transfer. The monopoly of lands was not always in response to purely economic factors. Dominions were not always extended to increase wealth, but in some instances to dominate, to be the lord and master of the region, like the "rich men" of Old Spain who were leaders and chiefs more than capitalists.

The country faced a depression toward the seventeenth century because of the reduction in the native population, who fell victim to the great epidemics, and the decline in mining due to the peninsular monopoly of mercury, bringing the country to near collapse. Everyone seemed to cling to his acquired positions, and thus were determined the characteristics of the great haciendas, which tended toward feudal forms of production. Great entailed estates

Santa Agueda. Vestibule of the big house. View from the second level.

Buenavista. Passageway connecting the chapel choir with the big house.

were consolidated, and limited commercial development contributed a patriarchal character to life on certain haciendas.

"These economic changes brought about other consequences: the disappearance of the *conquistador-encomendero,* the priest-evangelist, and the ethnic natives as central protagonists of the historic process. In the new economic and social configuration of the viceroyalty, the leadership role was now in the hands of merchants, miners, agriculturalists, and ranchers; the secular church; and the functionaries of the Crown. . . . In the seventeenth century, the Mexican countryside ceased to be an Indian countryside and became a mestizo countryside, a new countryside in which different ethnic groups created a new population and new ways of life."[9]

"In all these new forms of agricultural colonization, the master of the hacienda, the rancher, the proprietor of sugar plantations, and their legions of majordomos, overseers, administrators, cowboys, shepherds, and farmers constituted the leading group of new populations. Their social role in the rural environment was overwhelming and incontestable, and their power over workers and the indigenous communities was curbed only by priests and religious clerks. In all interior settlements, villages, and cities, they shared positions in the cabildo with merchants and civil servants."[10] Nevertheless, these lords and masters realized only slim incomes from their vast holdings, because this rural aristocracy did not preoccupy itself with the economic yield of their lands, mainly because, since the sixteenth century, these dominions had been heavily mortgaged to the benefit of the church, which received 5 percent of their annual income. Before the last third of the seventeenth century, the big privileged importers of commerce were multiplying their entitled estates, acquiring titles of nobility, constructing palaces and churches, and founding convents and colleges.

During the second half of the eighteenth century, this "equilibrium" found itself threatened. Although the native, mestizo, and creole populations grew rapidly, the growth in silver production, in the commerce that followed the strength of mining operations, and, finally, in agriculture and livestock production caught up with the development.

Opportunities increased because cities such as Mexico, Puebla, Guadalajara, and others grew and because mining centers like Guanajuato, Pachuca, and Zacatecas became cities. Freedom of commerce, and the fact that Veracruz was no longer the only port, favored trade. Abolition of the privileges in the trade with Europe in the years 1779 to 1789 obliged one part of the Mexican nobility that had benefited from the import business to augment their income from their haciendas and, consequently, to modify the structure of the same.

Toward the end of the eighteenth century, diverse laws regulated the work of the Indians and established their rights, as well as the obligations of employers. Punishments were severely prohibited, advances to the Indians of more than five pesos were prohibited, and accounts between proprietors and laborers were verified every four months. Indians were free to work wherever they chose. Laws of 1767 and 1789, the work of Viceroy Matías Gálvez, were strengthened to eliminate servitude for debts.

In 1804 the Spanish government secularized the mortgages of the church, with the intent of benefiting itself. This caused uneasiness and anger among the creole hacienda owners, many of whom came to embrace the cause of independence.

The mentality of the hacienda owner had become so deep-rooted that following independence, although large entitled estates and primogeniture were abolished, they failed to disappear and survived under the form of co-ownership.

"In the nineteenth century, the wars of independence and the civil wars tend to create a climate of insecurity, and the hacienda is often converted into a fortified place or refuge, and bodyguards and private armies reappear. As Don Luis Chávez Orozco notes, peons are given equal legal treatment as other citizens, thereby losing the benefits of protective laws, and debt peonage becomes widespread again."[11]

In 1856, one of the great Reform Laws, the Lerdo Law, decreed the expropriation of the great landholdings of the Catholic Church, with the aim of distributing the lands and creating a class of small independent farmers. However, since the property was put up for sale, only the rich hacienda owners were able to acquire it, augmenting their possessions and consolidating them into the great *latifundios*. "During the

Porfiriato, the policy of increasing the *latifundio* at the expense of the native communities was continued, as was observed in the issuing of the decree of December 15, 1893, and the law of March 26, 1894. The first authorized the creation of teams of surveyors to measure, divide, and evaluate vacant lands. . . . The results of the application of this decree were disastrous for the communities and the small proprietors, since they were unaccustomed to registering their titles, and unregistered properties were included within the 'vacant lands.' In this circumstance, the survey of the vacant lands turned into a means to concentrate landownership. Of the 38,249,377 hectares that had been surveyed by the year 1889, 12,693,980 hectares were given to the surveyors as payment and 14,681,980 hectares were sold at a very low price, and generally to friends of Díaz and members of his cabinet, leaving the nation only 12,300,000 hectares."[12]

To debt peonage, which was common in the country during the Porfiriato, we need to add that of leasing, which was widespread in the haciendas from the nineteenth century to the beginning of the twentieth. Through this system, with its marked traditional nature and precapitalist traits, lessees had use of the land according to the wishes of the hacienda owner, and in exchange for the parcel allotted to them by the owner as a lease, they paid him in labor or in kind with a share of their crop, with the excess destined for their own consumption. "To the foregoing types of labor should be added '*los meseros*,' a category of employees paid in money, though they also received additional payment in kind. These were essentially salaried employees who had the entire confidence of the hacienda owner and occupied positions essential to the organization."[13]

"The hacienda as a productive unit, intended from its beginning to produce goods for the local market, continued to fulfill this commercial role during the Porfiriato. The progressive consolidation of a capitalist economy in the Porfiriato provided the haciendas with expanded markets, increased production, and the consequent alteration of their internal structure."[14]

"The tendency toward a market economy that appeared at the end of the nineteenth century was favored by external demand, the establishment of railroads, and the suppression of internal tariffs. It's interesting to note that from 1892 to 1910 exports increased more than three times. The hacienda, as the producer of foodstuffs for domestic consumption, adapted partially to the Porfiriato economy, which continued adhering to market necessities while maintaining in large measure its traditional features. It resorted to the monopoly of landownership as a means of cornering the market for its products and to the utilization of the land and workforce, because of their abundance and reduced cost, rather than to the investment of capital to improve tools and techniques of cultivation."[15]

The *latifundios* survived the Revolution, although not with the same relationship to production, until the late thirties, when President Cárdenas passed the law of agrarian reform.

CHAPTER TWO

TWO

FORCES

TWO EXPRESSIVE FORCES are evident in hacienda architecture: one, intuitive and spontaneous, derives its impulse from the collective subconscious and from the common knowledge of a community (popular or vernacular architecture); the other, also deeply felt, is the product of the consciousness and vigor of the individual artist or of the great masters, of the creative academician or the intellectual endeavor of a single person (academic architecture). These two forces, spontaneous or not and of such distinct origin, converge in the architectural phenomenon of the hacienda, where harmony manifests itself.

Hassan Fathy refers to the former as ". . . the complete harmony between object, form, and the place where they meet, not only geographically but cosmically." He adds: "man battles against the contingencies of his culture and materials. It is a duel with matter, and when the problem is resolved, beauty is created. The object cannot possibly be ugly, since it could not be realized in any other way."[1]

Some architectural elements that are the product of popular culture are wells, pavements, granaries, *remates* and *coronamientos*, kitchens, housing for peons, mule corrals, water elements —simple, intelligible, functional architectural elements in perfect accord with the time and place. The constructions are mere pretext for what become examples of creative architecture. In effect, the spaces already formed engender sentiments and aspirations with which the proprietor never concerned himself.

Ravéreau, referring to representative archi-

Peotillos. Portal of the main patio.

tecture that reflects academic style and authority, says: "Order in architecture is the organization of elements into a constructed whole, apart from its functions. This organization depends upon laws, notions of composition such as unity, balance, proportional relationships, rhythms, axes, hierarchies, and symmetries— orders instituted through civilizations, often to comply with building programs."[2]

Tlalayote.
Façade of the big house.

*Chimalpa. Façade of the
big house.*

San Martín Notario. Entry to the pigsties.

La Noria. Side of the compound.

15

History teaches us about constructions where the purpose is representative. Simple architectural programs receive the influence of foreign models and are transformed in the search for a new interpretation. The satisfaction of seeing and fulfilling a vision becomes the desire for ostentation. The notion of the spectacular is manifested in a capricious architecture sustained by a gratuitous and temperamental will, deprived of the support of objective, geographic, constructive, and historical restrictions. The result is that many times the details fall within the category of contrivance—an architecture that emphasizes form and distances itself from its context, when it imports foreign models that are far removed from their cultural and autochthonous roots. Nevertheless, this strategy, in which expressive forces apply as standards in place of academic laws, has led to prodigious works.

Once again the hacienda reminds us of the convergence of these two expressive forces. It becomes a symbol that illustrates in a masterful way a long period of our past and attests to a search—the search for harmony.

Pozo del Carmen. Dam.

CHAPTER THREE

THE WORLD
OF THE HACIENDA
REFLECTED IN
ITS ARCHITECTURE

DIVERSE ACTIVITIES took place in the haciendas, each one with its corresponding space with distinct characteristics. This accounts for the architectural richness of the hacienda, which could accommodate the whole gamut of human endeavor: to harvest, to sing, to milk, to laugh, to cry, to pray, to die, to dream. . . .

The type of production of each hacienda contributed significantly to the architectural variety of the hacienda compound. There were pulque-extracting haciendas in Apan, henequen-growing ones in Yucatán, sugarcane cultivators in Morelos, cotton planters in La Laguna, stock raisers in the north, agricultural producers in Zacatecas, mescal cultivators in San Luis Potosí, grain growers in the Bajío (lowlands), and so on. The production of such a variety of products resulted in architectural elements characteristic of each: *tinacales*, sugar mills, silos, cowsheds, mule and burro pens, corrals, ovens, tanning vats, *chacuacos*, mills, and granaries. However, this is not to say that combinations of activities and elements did not occur, owing to the self-sufficient nature of the hacienda. Haciendas attracted workers from among Indian settlements, mestizos, and poor Spaniards, who saw them as an escape from poverty. The owner of the hacienda protected them in exchange for their labor.

This convivial relationship between proprietors and workers is reflected in constructions such as the big house, workers' quarters, *patio de campo*, company store, kitchens, chapel, and other outbuildings. In some haciendas, it was necessary to protect goods and people. This necessity was manifested in walls, towers with battlements, merlons, and loopholes. In the closed and self-sufficient world of the hacienda, people of diverse social origins were born, reared, and died: on one hand were the owners who possessed the lands and the means of production, and on the other were the workers who only possessed their strength for working. The differences between these two groups of people were evident in their manner of perceiving reality: despite being connected by a single religion, they had distinct traditions, varied by their pleasures, customs, and beliefs, and, above all, their different histories.

The landed gentry decided what constructions were needed, and the character of these depended upon their will. With utilitarian, practical, and functional intent that satisfied the basic requirements, without excesses, they ordered the construction of workers' quarters, granaries, and wells. On the other hand, in the spaces reserved exclusively for the use of the hacienda owner, his family, and his guests, we find foreign models, excesses, caprices, sophistications—everything that pertained to well-being, recreation, and comfort. There were also the luxuries, aesthetic pretensions, and generous resources spent on the "Divine Cult," which were expressed in chapels, the space shared by proprietors and workers.

As we saw earlier, the hacienda underwent changes from its origin until our time. These political, economic, social, and technological changes also affected the architectural manifestations of the institution. Such is the case with the modifications sustained by haciendas when their

Peñasco. Backyard.

proprietors decided to abandon stock raising, for example, and to convert their latifundium to farming or to dedicate it to the industrialization of some product in order to satisfy the demand of the national or export market. Such changes over time, whether gradual or accelerated in response to technological advances or social movements, left their imprint on the hacienda. Prosperity is reflected in the increase and complexity of irrigation works, the appearance of dams and new aqueducts. The big house is rebuilt, and storage spaces expand. The scale of the operation changes until the compound acquires its familiar dimensions; conforming to an eclecticism that is explained by the adaptations and expansions that corresponded to the tastes of the moment when they were realized.

In addition to the changes that were reflected in the architecture, the character and roles of the hacienda owner were seen in a marked distribution of spaces: those for work, living, recreation, and worship. Buildings that make up the whole of the hacienda are arranged sequentially from public spaces to the most private—those reserved for the owner, his family, and his guests. Areas serving as a backdrop for the relationship of the landowner and his workers, such as the office and the chapel, are strategically placed between public and private areas. This coexistence in a self-sufficient and ordered world is resolved in an ideal schema: one that allows all to work, live, play, and fulfill religious obligations. Nevertheless, as popular wisdom says, "together but not blended."

19

Pozo del Carmen. New house. Principal façade of the big house.

CHAPTER FOUR

THE

COMPOUND

HACIENDAS, spread over and integrated with the immense Mexican landscape, are of special interest because of their relationship to the natural environment. No traveler, past or present, can erase the always astonishing image of these massed buildings so typical of the architecture of rural Mexico. Climatic conditions of the haciendas we studied varied from the rocky aridity of San Luis Potosí, passing through the dry and temperate plains of Apan, to the quasi humidity of Tlaxcala. These varying climates determine the vegetation that surrounds the buildings and gives character to the image of each compound (*casco*). The terrain was taken into consideration in siting the compound. The choice of site, for practical or aesthetic reasons, differed in each case. Nevertheless, the harmonic relationship of the buildings with the lay of the land is a constant.

The hacienda of Santa María Tecajete is protected at the foot of a hill. La Ventilla dominates a valley from the top of a hill, and a river encircles the compound of Los Reyes. Tetlapaya climbs the foothills of a mountain, and the silhouette of the new house at Pozo del Carmen evokes mountain crests rising from an interminable plain.

Names given to haciendas also reveal this relationship of man to his natural environment: Peotillos, Tecajete (mortar, same as a *molcajete*), Montecillos (small hills), Peñasco (rock, crag), Bledos (wild amaranth), and Tepetates (a kind of stone employed in construction)—a straightforward and local relationship through which man and hacienda become rooted in the landscape.

It is important to mention the suggestion made by George Kubler (an authority on Mexican architecture of the sixteenth century), in his book published in 1948, concerning the link between the Mexican hacienda and its historical antecedents in southern Spain. "This example imitated, perhaps, the great Andalusian farm-estates of the sixteenth and seventeenth centuries in Seville and Córdoba, with their high perimeter walls, ample patios, sumptuous entrances, and numerous outbuildings. . . . Regardless, the great haciendas of the nineteenth century in Mexico have a long history, and it should not be difficult to establish a connection between the Arabic *al-muniat* (large orchard or vegetable garden) of southern Spain, the farm-estates of Andalusia, and these latifundia of the nineteenth century."[1]

The architect Fernando García Mercadal, a student of popular Spanish architecture, states: "The Andalusian farm-estate is the dwelling of the master of the grand latifundium, around

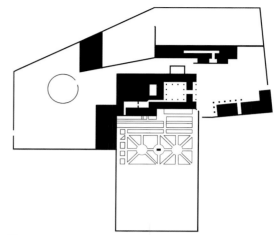
Totoapa.

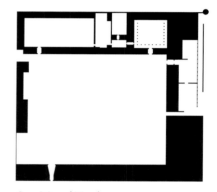
San Miguel Tepalca.

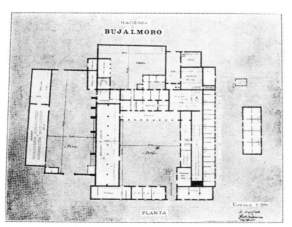
Bujalmoro.

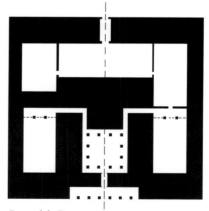
Pozo del Carmen.

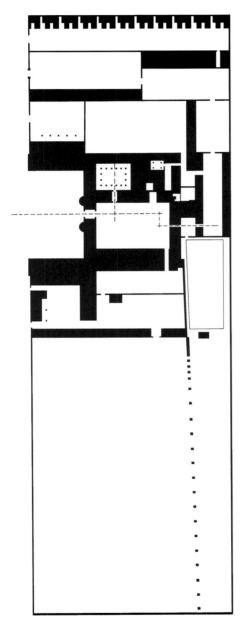

Tecajete.

Ciénega de Mata. View of the compound.

which are grouped those of the day-laborers and salaried workforce, plus those of all the locals needed for cultivating the land. . . . The base is the big patio or uncovered space, closed in front by a wall with a great gate and on the other sides by rural buildings: the house of the operator, manager, or foreman; habitations of the employees; stables; cowsheds; warehouses; granaries. . . . In many cases, there are multiple patios. The buildings, generally single-story, are plain in appearance, but with unmistakable features. In this type, one senses the Roman tradition of grouping buildings around uncovered spaces."[2]

Compounds of the Mexican haciendas were also defined by the farm buildings. Within the compound were grouped the big house, the chapel, structures for processing or storing agricultural products—granaries, *tinacales*, storerooms, mescal-processing buildings, mills, stables, mule pens, pigsties, corrals, silos—workers' houses, workshops, and other outbuildings. In some cases, these buildings were surrounded by high walls that set apart the workers' quarters. Such walls were pierced by an impressive entrance, called the "*puerta de campo*," which was protected by towers that gave to the whole the aspect of an imposing fortress. In other cases the buildings were organized around a plaza. Here were the big house, the chapel, granaries, cowsheds, workers' quarters, and other outbuildings distributed along streets without any enclosing walls.

This phenomenon was also linked to different productions and regional differences: among the haciendas we studied, the walled compounds were associated with the extraction of pulque and were found in the plains of Apan; the unwalled ones are in San Luis Potosí and were dedicated to producing mescal, grains, and livestock. A similar example is found in Tlaxcala, where much smaller haciendas than those of San Luis Potosí developed agricultural production with no walls surrounding the compound. In either case, walled or not, the complex groups its buildings around a large *patio de campo* or plaza. Each edifice, in turn, is organized in a succession of *zaguanes* and patios that also evoke the Andalusian tradition and, earlier still, the presence of Arabic architecture.

On this subject, García Mercadal states that "the Mohammedan tradition is observed principally in the alternative varieties of passageways and patios, with their corresponding effects of light and color. Their gradation tends to be: entrance, work patio, passageway, principal patio, house of the proprietor, and garden."[3] Another similarity with the architecture of Andalusian farms is found in the conventual

Tetlapaya. View of the compound.

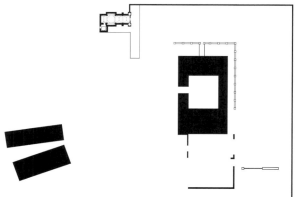

Los Reyes.

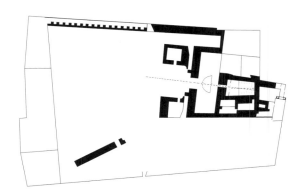

Mazaquiahuac.

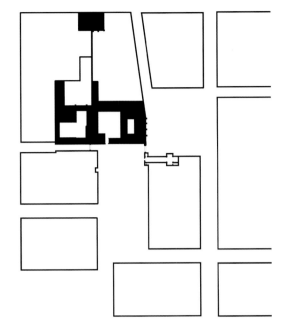

Bledos.

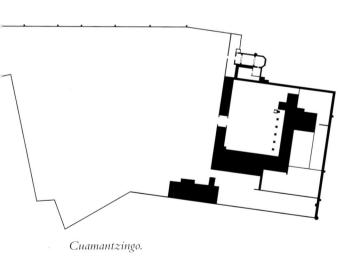

Cuamantzingo.

aspect of many of the compounds we studied—not a few of which were the property of religious orders. These congregations imprinted their mark to the point of making them resemble their *conventos*. This was also observed by Gutiérrez Moreno, the premier authority on the history of the popular architecture of Andalusia, when he says: "These massed buildings seem like monasteries. Their towers, crowned with crosses, contribute to that impression, as does their principal entrance, where there is always a religious image on the coat of arms."[4]

The hacienda was a work place, a residence, a place of leisure, and of religion. This union of human endeavor, in an institution where landowners and employees coexisted in a closed and self-sufficient world, had as its primary stage the compound. In the schema of the compound, these functions are manifested as a constant order that persists, that does not vary, despite the different possibilities of combination. This general plan, which covers everything from work, to recreation, to worship, materializes in this manner: a *patio de campo* or plaza defined by granaries, workers' quarters, chapel, and big house. The work patio precedes a second patio, closed on all four sides, which in turn orders the habitations and patios that constitute the big house. This residence of the proprietor extends into orchards and gardens, settings for recreation.

Spaces and volumes of the compound combine in various ways, but always in accordance with this plan. The *patio de campo*, that great space with multiple functions, is contained in some cases by walls and buildings and acquires diverse forms. In other examples, it surrounds the buildings, containing and embracing their volumes. Buildings in the hacienda of San Miguel Tepalca are grouped around a great patio, and the organization of space is quite clear, whereas in the hacienda of Los Reyes, the structures rise loosely in a great space, which can only be called a "*patio de campo*" because of its functions. However, both solutions appear in combination at times. Some *patios de campo* are partially surrounded by walls and buildings, while other sections open onto streets or face cultivated fields unimpeded by structures. Such is the case of the haciendas of Bledos, Peotillos, or La Ventilla, where the workers' houses, granaries, stores, and workshops are organized around the great plaza to form a *patio de campo* from which emerge streets and paths that end in the cultivated fields, thus giving the compound the look of a pueblo.

Up to this point we have discussed the *patio de campo*, which is the largest space in all the complexes. Like it, other patios with smaller dimensions reproduce the organizing function of the buildings so clearly that we can consider "the patio" as the theme inherent in this architecture. In the haciendas we studied, one sees three scales used in patios, depending upon the activities pursued there. By far the largest one in terms of size is the *patio de campo*. In diminishing scale follow those corresponding to mule pens, stables, pigsties, or, sometimes, workers' quarters, and lastly, the principal patio of the big house, with its private patios that precede the

Cuamantzingo.
View of the compound.

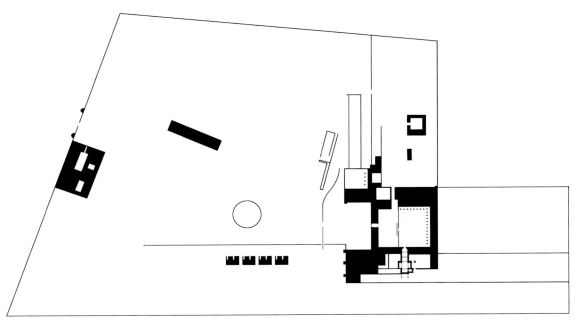

Tetlapaya.

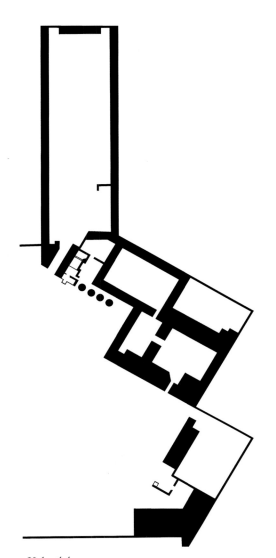

Xalpatlahuaya.

orchards and gardens. Whatever the pertinent scale, each patio organizes the structures that surround it, and its regularity predominates over the variety of volumetric forms.

A variety of elements contribute to the regularity of patios. Rhythm and symmetry are evident in their porticos and columns, in the placement of their trees, in the design of their paved surfaces, and in the location of their benches and fountains. The possible movement through these patios permits us to grasp their theme and its sequences. Indeed, the succession of open spaces is a constant in all the layouts, even though the sequence takes on different directions. There are patios that present a single axis, others that follow discontinuous ones, and still others that abandon an axis in order to spread out and give us the sensation of virtual labyrinths.

In the plans of the haciendas studied, an orthogonal organization was used where topography permitted. Thus, natural obstacles generate twists of greater or lesser importance, as in the cases of Xalpatlahuaya and La Ventilla, where the residences of the administrator and other trusted employees were situated on an elevated site and rotated in respect to the rest of the buildings. Another interesting case is that of the deviations seen in the *tinacal* and granaries of Totoapa, which follow the course of the river without forgetting the orthogonal intention that dominates the whole.

Tetlapaya. Portal.

Venta de Cruz. Zaguán.

Symmetry is present in hacienda architecture even though it does not characterize it. Nevertheless, in all examples one observes axes of composition, which with greater or lesser force organize the volumes. In some cases, they are quite evident, as in the new house of Pozo del Carmen or in Mazaquiahuac. In others, as in Tecajete or La Ventilla, the axes can only be partially recognized in discrete areas of the whole.

The concept of a sole focal point is absent in all the compounds, except for the chapel, which always follows the architectural alignment of Western religious architecture. The importance of the buildings and the relationship between them is intimately linked to the functions that the hacienda played as an institution in the society. Agricultural production, the primary function of the haciendas we studied, is evident in the size and importance of the spaces allotted to the storage of the related products. The owner's residence, the big house, imposes itself by facing the quarters designated to house the workers and their families. Finally, the faith shared by all the inhabitants of the compound also has its setting, its place of worship, in the chapel, which always stands out due to its specific characteristics.

Tepalca. Zaguán.

Tecajete. Zaguán *leading to the stables*.

Peñasco. Zaguán.

The horizontality of the big house, which is repeated at a lesser height in the workers' quarters, always contrasts with the verticality of the chapel, accentuated by towers, cupolas, and *espadañas*.

The architectural ordering of the owner's house and the church, always in proximity to one another, is clear. However, in the structures of granaries, silos, or *tinacales*, whether free-standing or annexed to the house, it is evident in all haciendas that pure geometric forms predominate. Their volume is such that when they are situated on both sides of the entryway to the house, they form wings that embrace a large part of the *patio de campo*, indicating access to the most important residence in the hierarchy—as one can appreciate principally in haciendas of the pulque-producing area.

As we already mentioned, the hierarchy of these storage spaces is related to their function and purpose. In the same manner, this phenomenon is present in conventual architecture of the sixteenth century, where buildings also acquired hierarchies determined by the institution. In *conventos*, chapels and their atria are enormous compared with areas intended for habitation or storage of crops—which is to be expected in an institution so strictly linked to the task of evangelization. By contrast, the institutional purpose of the hacienda is reflected in the areas devoted to housing the produce and tools, and the animals and human beings that made it all possible.

Socoyucan.
Portal.

CHAPTER FIVE

THE

BIG HOUSE

THE BIG HOUSE is always found in the *patio de campo*, and its unmistakable presence faces the visitor across a large expanse between the observer and its principal façade. In all cases, the lay of the land, the existence of walls, or the position of other constructions of the compound creates obstacles and passages so that the initial visual contact is the front of the owner's residence. Lateral or back façades are blind or have only the openings necessary for those within, without regard to the visual effect of the exterior. In some cases, volumes attached to the house obstruct the view of the principal façade, save in cases where there is a front garden to which access is less direct.

The front façade of the big house is always emphasized, with other buildings of the compound subordinate to it. When the house is isolated, its principle façade makes use of porticos and ornate elements that emphasize the entrance. The use of other structures to integrate and emphasize the façade is effected in several ways. Such is the case of chapels that are linked by bridges, arcades, or loggias, thus

Tecajete, Hidalgo.
Living Room.

BELOW: *Tecajete.*

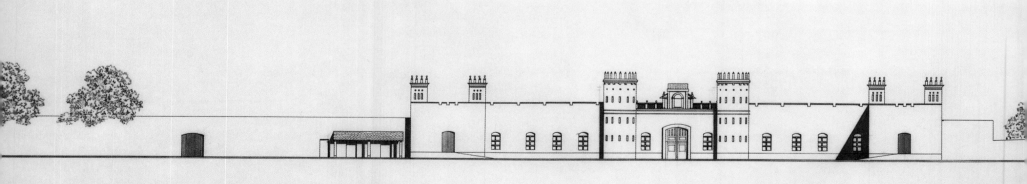

Tecajete.
Dining Room

BELOW RIGHT: *Tecajete.*

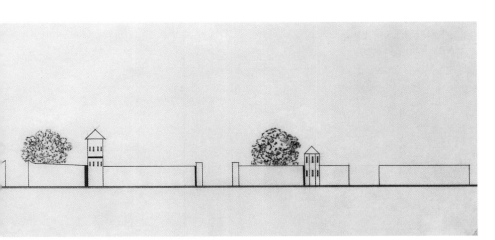

achieving a composition that exalts the whole. Other examples are granaries and *tinacales*, unambiguously attached to the house, that serve as enormous vestibular entrances to the principal door.

The same results are achieved with edifices of less volumetric importance that lineally and modestly add to the presence of a frontispiece of great richness. Flanking the principal entry—always unmistakable due to its importance and scale—are benches, either in the open or under the porches, that accentuate the necessity of keeping the stranger out of the house. Behind this entry awaits a *zaguán* where other wooden benches extend the anteroom for the visitor, who is allowed no farther than the office to preserve the privacy of the proprietor's family.

In the schema of patios already mentioned, *zaguanes* fulfill functions of movement and linkage between open spaces. They, like patios, differ in scale according to their use. The first *zaguán*, for example, has greater dimensions that permit the entry of people on horseback or in carriages. This is the norm, even when access to the stables and coach house is located in the *patio de campo*. In these cases, this *zaguán* connects to the outside by means of a patio

RIGHT: *Peotillos, Portal of the main patio.*

Peotillos.

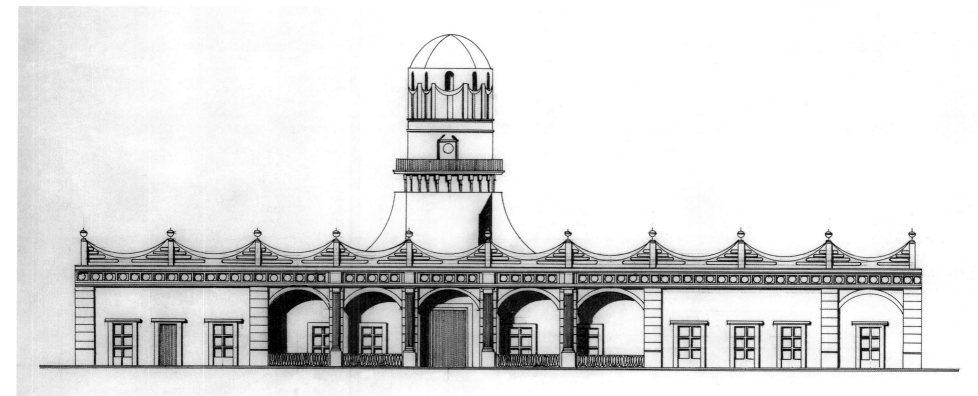

with accesses to habitations, stables, or coach houses and affords diverse solutions of levels, ramps, stairs, and pavements.

The *zaguán* leading to the principal patio, which sometimes is the first, acquires its distinctiveness from the dimensions of the building wing it passes through. When the wing is very wide, the *zaguán* is shorter and shares its function with portals connecting the outside and inside of the house, although this solution is not repeated on the upper story when there is one. In the main patio, the orthogonal plan is evident despite the combinations of porches, which range from total absence, as in Tenejac, to those that display them along one, two, three, or four sides. In all cases the patios are square, and they organize the volumes, always in succession, with certain constants. In most single-story houses, the wing opposite the entrance *zaguán* accommodates the dining room, while those on the sides are divided into living areas, and the front one is used for other rooms and the office. Where there are two stories, the staircase is often placed opposite the *zaguán* or dominates one side of the patio. In any case, the hierarchical solution par excellence for the patio is the entryways; where they occur, reflecting the taste and wealth of the owner, their architectural style relies upon the site's timber and stone to form arches or lintels.

In the main patio, the presence or absence of trees, plants, fountains, walks, and paving always obeys a design more evident than in other patios. It is a careful design that responds to the multiple uses and habits practiced in this attractive enclosure that has the sky as its roof and a topography indicative of zones differentiated by their conception and use. In these constructions where the patio is the theme and the plot, the general character of the hacienda, as well as the most individual character, manifests itself to make the patios of each house unique and unmistakable.

It is no wonder that the design of uncovered spaces is more sophisticated than the criterion that defines the living spaces along the corridors. Even the openings are arranged to achieve the effects of rhythm and hierarchy from the outside, while meeting the needs within. In the principal patio, with its entryways and paving, the paths emphasize directions broken in such a manner that no one can cross it arbitrarily without being aware of its presence, space, and time. In the main patio are doors accessing the living areas, at times the stairway leading to the upper porches and corridors, and *zaguanes* that beckon with their bright promise to other patios. By whichever path one leaves the main patio, the house will offer surprises, but the most astonishing of

Bledos. Kitchen.

BELOW: *Bledos.*

Ciénega de Mata.
Detail of the archway in the main patio.

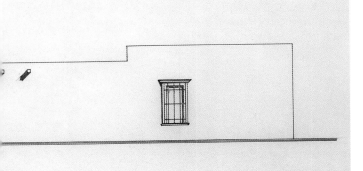

these will always be the manipulation of covered spaces to serve those open to the sky.

The patio is the landscape created by man, whether to refresh himself in or to enjoy from the dark rooms of this enclosed world that looks toward the light at its core, its very essence. Thus, in spite of changes wrought by time, the big house preserves the patio plan in order to organize spaces of unchanging quality that we can recognize and group according to their functions. These are the spaces assigned to the dining room, kitchen, bedrooms, living room, and office, which, though the house may be in ruins, can be identified by their dimensions, design, and location.

The rectangular dining room is always the largest room in the house and faces the main patio on one of its long sides. The opposing side may have either windows overlooking gardens and another patio or niches that mirror the openings facing the principal patio. The niches house china, dumbwaiters, or doors leading to the kitchens. In the majority of cases, one observes another room, the pantry, where food is served from the pots into serving dishes and platters. This room prevents the noise, smoke, and odors of the kitchen from disturbing the meal.

In two-story houses, the dining room is situated above, as is the kitchen, which is accessed from a service patio with its own staircase. Access to a patio with water troughs, ovens, charcoal bins, and sinks is characteristic of kitchens, where sun and air are always necessary to carry out some phases of processing

food: washing, plucking, drying in the sun, aerating, and so on.

Inside, the kitchen walls incorporate niches and reliefs, the combination of which results in a play of purely geometric forms and sculptural effects. This sensation is accentuated by the colors and textures of finishings and by the contrasts between light and shadow that make the kitchen area unique and unmistakable. The function that these elements offer, likewise unique and characteristic, is reflected in the ranges, chimney hoods, drafts, and fireboxes where the fire is lit and rekindled and the heat and smoke controlled. The *metate* and *comal* are found in their natural setting in kitchens of the hacienda, and it is quite easy to recognize in them the place set aside for milling the cornmeal and making tortillas.

On the other hand, and in frank contrast to the architectural richness of the kitchens, are the rooms designed for rest, reading, sleep, personal grooming, music, conversation, embroidering, or meditating, which in their design and realization lack any major constructed elements that apply to the functions for which they were intended. The rooms have high ceilings, orthogonal form, bare walls, and monotonous entries and apertures that are limited to communicating, illuminating, and ventilating without any great sophistication. The sheer number of rooms means that, taken together, they constitute the greater part of the total volume of the house. When the rooms that surround the principal patio failed to meet the spatial needs of the family and their relatives, new corridors were attached to the older ones. Then, in order to illuminate and ventilate these blocks of rooms, the plan of the patio appears once again to have fulfilled its task of ordering and integrating the volumes.

Communication between rooms was achieved through openings placed in the same direction, and these allowed inside access through simple circulation. The dimensions and number of these rooms clearly reflect the spatial requirements of the inhabitants of the house and the ideas and resources of the owners to satisfy them. The big house occupies a minimal portion of the total area of the property, but it is always in keeping with the size of the lati-fundium and the economic importance of each hacienda. Furthermore, the habitations reflect the conception of space—a generous conception that allowed for the sheltering of these large families, their relatives, their visitors, who, because of the isolation and distance, were obliged to spend the night in the house, and the more or less permanent guests.

Gogorrón. Side façade of the big house.

BELOW: *Los Reyes.*

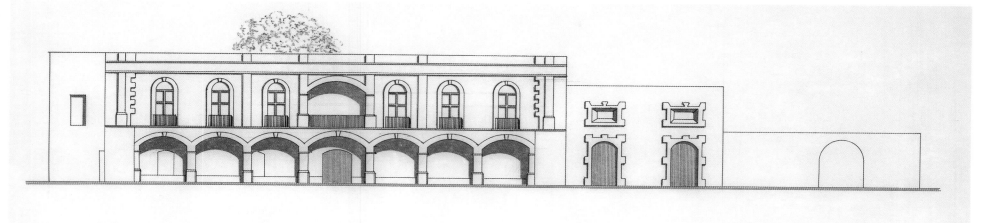

Gogorrón. Zaguán.

Pozo del Carmen.
Old house.

Tenejac. Main patio.

Peñasco.

Bocas.

Pozo del Carmen.

Pozo del Carmen. New House. Dining Room.

La Gavia. Living room.

TOP RIGHT: *La Gavia.*
Bedroom.

RIGHT: *Montecillos.*
Kitchen.

The concept of space also arose from the lifestyle of these people so used to enormous beds, wardrobes, armoires, tables, and chests that differ so much in function and size from those in use today.

Among the rooms we have just discussed, we have not mentioned the living room and office, since both have some architectural features that distinguish them from the rest. In the case of the living room, it is its size and, at times, its fireplace that characterize it. The office and the living room have something in common: they are generally situated on either side of the *zaguán*, in the same corridor, and their windows face the *patio de campo* and across the gate when there are two blocks of rooms. Other windows of these rooms face the main patio and, even in the case of living rooms situated on the upper floor, this double view to both the interior and exterior of the house is always possible, as if the owners were making apparent their desire that visitors maintain, in the office and living room, their link to the outside world associated with work, possession, and wealth while simultaneously affording them a peek into the private, intimate, and

exclusive world of the family and its closest circle.

As we have already said, the most conscious, thoughtful, rich, and distinctive architectural design was concentrated in the big house and the chapel. It is the house of the owner that reflects fashions, economic prosperity, and influences. Nevertheless, in this residence there are elements more susceptible than others to modifications. These occur with the greatest frequency in the principal façade that displays different styles, sometimes combined in disagreeable eclecticism. These façades are in stark contrast to interior ones—those that front the gardens and orchards, where they retain the values of popular, more traditional and harmonic architecture congruent with the rest of the house. A walk through the big house, full of the agreeable surprises offered by the plan of the patio, always ends in the orchards and gardens. These walled spaces contain roads, paths, fountains, cisterns, water-ways, bridges, and pavilions where one is able to enjoy vegetation that is varied and different from the native flora. Beyond the walls is the countryside, with its magueys, mesquites, grasses, and *pirules*. Within the walls are the ash trees, jasmines, fruit trees, cypresses, rose bushes, and cedars that grow in the microclimate created by man in order to enjoy a domesticated nature, selected and imported—a nature in stark contrast to the natural flora outside the walls and one supported and contained by beautiful constructed elements that the hacienda owners had at their service.

La Ventilla.
Main patio.

CHAPTER SIX

THE

CHAPEL

SINCE CATHOLICISM is intimately linked to the national identity, the Mexican institution of the hacienda naturally accommodated a chapel. Within these great properties, where proprietors and peons lived together, religion played a role in birth and death, in work and joy, in sadness and its consolation, in obligation, and in duty and hope. In all the haciendas we studied, there is an area set aside for worship, a place where owners and laborers with their families attended Catholic services and demonstrated their faith in shared beliefs.

Hacienda chapels always form part of the compound and are located close to the big house, when not forming part of it, as in the cases of San Francisco Soltepec, San Miguel Tepalca, and Tetlapaya. Wherever they are located, chapels imitate the characteristics of

Bledos.

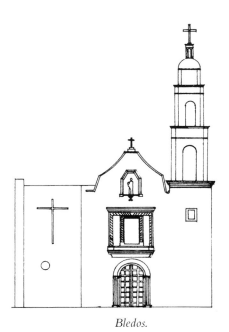

Bledos.

Pozo del Carmen.

religious architecture seen in *conventos*, towns, and cities of our country. From the sixteenth to the early twentieth century, all styles are present. However, on haciendas these characteristics are replicated on a domestic scale. In examples where this was not followed, as in Tetlapaya or Pozo del Carmen, the large scale was due to these haciendas being the property of religious orders. And, understandably, these owners had to offer services to a more extensive community than the one living within the compound. The dimensions of chapels, as well as their more or less architectural richness, were related to the number of workers on the hacienda and, in great measure, to the abilities and desires of the owner to manifest his religious sentiments.

In all chapels there is an attempt to reflect the

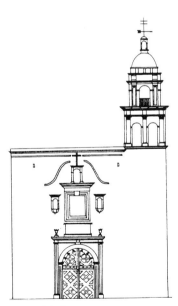

Pozo del Carmen.

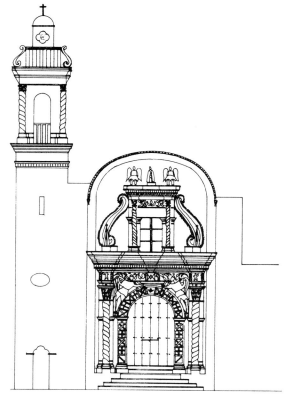

Tetlapaya.

Los Reyes.

Mazaquiahuac.

faith on the exterior and to sanctify the open space, a phenomenon that characterizes Mexican religious architecture. As in other churches, those of the haciendas include atria of different scale and location, but they always delimit the sacred space, even in terrain where it is abundant, and associate it very clearly to the religious structure. Atria are defined by low walls, which increase in height at an entry situated exactly opposite the church door. At this entry one observes the change in elevation of the church preceded by its paved atrium, which distinguishes it from the exterior space. In some cases,

one sees other lateral spaces at the same level set aside for the cemetery, where the dead repose in sacred ground. Gravestones, sculptures, crosses, and monuments of marble or cut stone are memorials to the owners and their families. Humble and impermanent stick crosses preserve for a short time the memory of the peons who ended their days in the hacienda.

Life and celebration also had a setting in these spaces where they honored the patron saint, prayed for rain, or gave thanks for good harvests. Each chapel was dedicated to the veneration associated with the patron saint of

Peotillos.

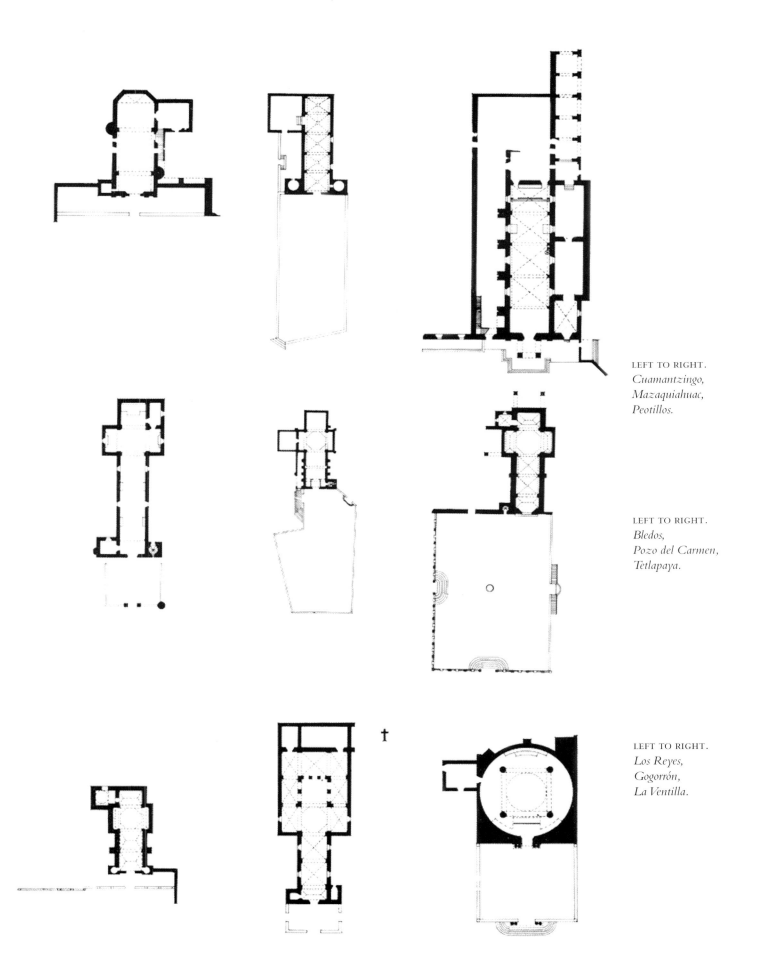

LEFT TO RIGHT.
Cuamantzingo,
Mazaquiahuac,
Peotillos.

LEFT TO RIGHT.
Bledos,
Pozo del Carmen,
Tetlapaya.

LEFT TO RIGHT.
Los Reyes,
Gogorrón,
La Ventilla.

TOP, LEFT TO RIGHT:
*Peotillos, La Ventilla, Pozo
del Carmen.* BOTTOM,
LEFT TO RIGHT:
Los Reyes, Tetlapaya.

the whole hacienda: to St. Mary in Tecajete, to St. James in Tetlapaya, to St. Peter in Gogorrón, or to the Virgin of Carmen in the hacienda del Pozo that bears her name.

This scene for devotion resulted in three types of plan: the single nave, the Latin cross, and, rarely, a central plan. By whatever type of plan, chapels were roofed with arches and vaults. In the case of cruciform plans, which finish their crossing with a cupola, the latter is almost always octagonal. In the hacienda of La Ventilla, the only chapel we studied with a central plan, its cupola made use of a circular drum, in Renaissance style.

The size of the chapels and the resources allocated to them determined the choice of roofing: barrel vaults or simple beamed flat roofs. Windows were always placed high and on side walls. Although infrequent, they are sufficient to provide subtle illumination, which, supplemented with candlelight, encouraged meditation, devoutness, and respect.

The number of bays in the nave varies from two to five. This determines the proportions of each church without disregarding typical plan organization. The choir is located in the first bay; the apse in the last, and the crossing in the one preceding it. The main altar and reredos are placed in the rectangular or polygonal apse. Other altar pieces and the pulpit are arranged along the walls of the nave before the main altar and crossing. In the transepts are secondary altars and, sometimes, the tombs of the owners. Doors to the sacristy are found either in the apse or in one of the transepts. Doors accessing the choir are at a higher level, reflecting the hierarchy that separated the people of the big house from their workers. The owners, who arrived directly from the house to the chapel via loggias, doors, or passages, observed the service from the choir or a simple balcony. Others entered through the big door and occupied the larger spaces of less importance. Sometimes an interior staircase led to the choir and rose to the bell tower. In other examples, separate staircases led to each.

Chapels elevated their towers or *espadañas* to contrast with the horizontality of other build-ings. As at Gogorrón, some had two towers, while at others, such as Totoapa, bells were hung from *espadañas* that vary from simple to complex. The principal door is framed and surrounded with ornate elements that reflect, on the one hand, the fashion and time, and on the other, popular taste and sentiment. Materials, whether local or imported, are carved, molded, stuccoed, gessoed, and painted to embellish niches, *remates,* arches, reliefs, oculi, pediments, columns, cornices, and images.

In these façades, the taste, wealth, devotion, and spiritual interest of the owners are present. The sentiments of the artisans are likewise expressed, along with their desire to achieve harmony and beauty. Nevertheless—and this happened in some churches of the nineteenth century—the standards and dominant authority for imposing them led to one or another absurdity that only attracts the eye because of its extravagance.

Side façades owe their character to buttresses, flying buttresses, and sometimes a staircase, which add to the rhythm of their volumes. Their character is also enhanced by the purity of their lines and the textures of diverse materials stripped of carvings and stucco, ready to receive their color from water, air, and time. We said that in the big house the principal façade was the area most vulnerable to modifications.

In chapels, this phenomenon occurs more often in interior decoration, which at times surprises us with neoclassic workmanship or neo-Gothic details in wood that contrast with the folk tradition of a Mexican façade. In the most fortunate examples, where the interior has not suffered plundering, robbery, or vandalism, the baroque richness of the façade is repeated in the reredos. Their forms acquire brilliancy and different textures when the gilded and polychromed images are well illuminated.

While it is true that modifications compromised the unity and harmony of these churches, their sacred nature preserved them from abandonment. In the examples in which the entire compound is in ruins, the chapel remains standing—thanks to the care given to them by the unassuming faithful. The hacienda is disappearing as an institution, obsolete and irreconcilable with the Mexico of today, but religion persists to the present in the hearts of the peasants (now themselves the owners of small plots of land) who preserve the Catholic faith, the religion that formerly reconciled the owners and peons who lived and died in the hacienda.

CHAPTER SEVEN

SPACES

FOR

PRODUCTION

THE IMMENSE LANDS of the latifundium—whether seeded, reserved for pastures, filled with enormous mineral or forest wealth, or deserted and uncultivated—constituted the support or base of all production. The hacienda was, above all else, a productive unit. Most buildings erected to fulfill this function were located in the compound: granaries that stored the harvest, *tinacales* where pulque was extracted, and sheds for the reproduction of livestock. From the proportionate size of each building in relation to the rest, we are able to determine where the weight of exploitation fell in these self-sufficient yet diversified units. We have grouped our observations about these constructions according to the activities and products related to them: grains, livestock, pulque and mescal.

In order to store grain harvests, threshing floors, granaries, and silos were constructed. Threshing floors were situated in the *patio de campo*, and their circular form makes them unmistakable in the plans of the compound. All have flagstone paving and are demarcated with approximately one-meter-high walls that keep the animals from leaving the threshing site.

Silos, subterranean places where dried grains were stored, appear at the surface as conical or cylindrical volumes rooted on a circular base. Their only access, and at times their only window, does not detract from their pure geometric forms.

Granaries or corn lofts are constructed of rubble stone, adobe, or cut stone. They are rectangular and have a single entrance. The

Buenavista. Granary.

La Ventilla. Granary.

windows are small and open under the eaves of the roof. There are larger granaries located apart or grouped so as to constitute a single volume. Occasionally they are attached to the big house and, as in some haciendas in Tlaxcala, they are accessed from the main patio. Aside from these enormous buildings, we find smaller ones that fulfill the same function on a domestic scale; there are always granaries for grains and fodder in the vicinity of the animal sheds, stables, or mule pens and other similar areas that serve the big house.

Over time, granaries were built following the same designs. Thus, it is difficult to establish on the basis of their style in which century they were built, since the same materials and solutions recur. Within these constants, we can distinguish two types of granaries: those with two aisles with center supports of arches and columns, and those with a single aisle with exterior buttresses or support achieved by means of the thickness of the walls. In the first, the space is divided by the central support. If this is an arcade, access is in the side walls or to one side of the buttress that receives the thrust. If support is through columns or pilasters with lintels, the door occurs at the center.

Granaries are rectangular because other forms could not provide the large volume of storage space needed. Those of a single aisle often have two or three levels with flat-roofed or vaulted mezzanines. In this case, the buttresses are more sophisticated, such as the flying buttresses that we see in the granaries of La Ventilla. The height of the walls, added to

Gogorrón. Granary.

Santa Agueda. Granary.

Peñasco. Mescal factory.

Zotoluca. Inside the tinacal.

Zotoluca. Tinacal.

Tetlapaya.
Interior of the tinacal.

Segura.
Granary.

the rectangular shape of the plan, produce these formidable tunnels covered with barrel vaults or gable roofs.

These interior spaces receive light through the small, pure geometric forms of the windows, whether oval, rectangular, or square. The dimly lit accumulated wealth, retaining all the smells of the field, is illuminated briefly in the small areas where the last rays of light die. This intimate world, protected from all natural inclemencies and all human and animal damage, stands firm with these impressive, invulnerable constructed masses that have resisted the assault of time. Even today these granaries constructed in colonial times are still used. The spontaneous, popular, and modest ornamental details further underscore the importance of these structures that hide and protect the harvest so well. But one guesses at the wealth within from the sheer size of these granaries, in spite of their architectural austerity.

Constructions intended for animals are also situated in the compound, strategically kept some distance from the house in order to avoid the annoyances of odors, pests, and insects that their proximity would cause. These buildings can be classified according to the animals for which they were designed. There are pens for mules; cowsheds for bovines; corrals for small animals such as sheep, goats, turkeys, and hens; and stables for fine riding animals. The dimensions of these constructions depended upon the number of animals kept by the hacienda. They too were arranged around a patio conceived for the multiple activities required for the management of each species. In these patios, cattle were killed, castrated, and branded; horses were shod and bathed; sheep were sheared; young bulls were lassoed; and colts were broken.

Mule pens, porticoed structures with columns or pillars, were attached to a wall with an inclined tile roof that shed rain toward the patio. At the end were located feeding troughs made of rubble stone, and watering troughs stood in the open air.

Cowsheds, stalls with gable roofs and paired columns, lacked side walls and sheltered their feeding troughs in the center. These stalls, where milking also occurred, were arranged around a patio or were parallel to one another and had a stone-paved corridor for the movement of animals. Corrals were unroofed, and their construction was limited to feeding troughs and the posts that supported the fence. Such enclosures were always situated in proximity to other roofed buildings to facilitate the transfer of some animal that needed to be protected from the inclemencies of weather, as in the case of valuable breeding stock, those that were wounded or sick, a female about to give birth, or a newborn orphan that had to be fed artificially.

Stables were the most conspicuous buildings intended for animals. And this is no wonder, since the horse was the animal most prized by the hacienda owners. It was their means of transportation, used as a draft and work horse, or ridden for pleasure. But above all, their mounts made clear the mastery of the owners,

San Lorenzo. Tinacal.

Pozo del Carmen.
Stables.

La Concordia. Noria.

who could ride around their property and oversee from on high their peons, who were always on foot or, on occasion, on burros.

In stables we find barrel-vaulted roofs, high stone walls, window frames of cut stone, and ornamented and skillfully finished columns and arches. The patio that organizes the stables also takes on a distinct quality, with its rhythmic fenestration, stone-paving design, wall color, and pure geometry in the drinking troughs. There are two types of stables: those with interior stalls in an enormous area, and those in which the stalls are aligned under semi-enclosed portals with direct access to the patio. From the big house, one was always easily able to reach these places where the horses were kept in such comfort. Also found in these patios were the special granaries for fodder, large tack rooms, and carriage houses where valuable horse equipment and carriages were kept.

For the manufacture of pulque they used *tinacales*, which, with their own special characteristics, equaled the volumetric and hierarchical dimensions of granaries. Whether freestanding or attached to the big house, *tinacales* utilized the same material and technical resources of other buildings. Nevertheless, the unique nature of pulque, long used by Mesoamerican people, marks the *tinacal* as something singularly Mexican, as do the magueys from which the drink is made and which so particularly mark the rural countryside of the high plains.

The commercialization of pulque is tightly linked to the means of transporting it rapidly and efficiently to the centers of consumption. It is for this reason that its boom coincides with the modernization of the country and the appearance of the railroad. During this epoch many haciendas change their course: seeded fields are replaced with magueys, and granaries are converted to *tinacales*. In other cases, the economic prosperity of the new enterprise is reflected in *tinacales* constructed by professionals and in modifications and expansions made to the big house and the chapel.

In contrast to the granary, the *tinacal* was constructed with the intent of creating an interior environment suited to a production that possesses ritualistic characteristics.[1] Openings controlled light and ventilation and maintained coolness. Its beams, cupolas, or high vaults evoked the ambience of a church. *Tinacales* with octagonal or circular plans, made at the end of the last century and at the beginning of the twentieth, benefited from their siting apart from the rest of the buildings of the compound and stand out due to their ostentatious design, so typical of the era, which also incorporated the tastes and composition of façades and the interiors of chapels. These *tinacales*, conceived from neo-Gothic, neoclassic, and neo-Arabic styles of composition, had surprising results in the haciendas: by combining marble sculptures, pointed arches, and acanthus volutes with leather vats, gourd dippers, calabash cups, and graters, the outer ambience shelters a straightforward, popular, and very Mexican form.

Popular sentiment is expressed on their walls, and the frescoes address simple country

Tetlapaya.
Worker's house.

TOP: *Tetlapaya.*
Workers' quarters.

64

Peotillos.
Noria.

65

scenes. But there are also paintings congruent with the romantic and pretentious architectural intent that places herons, nymphs, and cupids on the walls—condemned to be impregnated with the unmistakable odor that always reminds us of the earth and our roots.

Just as the haciendas of the plains of Apan were devoted to the production of pulque, those of San Luis Potosí produced mescal. Though this industry is important, it does not contribute as much to the wealth of the hacienda as is the case with pulque. Even so, this activity required a setting, which, because of its dimensions, has significant value within the architecture. These extensive complexes, generally roofed with barrel vaults, had spaces to house the different stages in producing mescal liquor. These activities call for very definite and different elements. The simplicity, size, functional qualities, and tectonic rigor realized in these works arouse intense feelings that the viewer cannot ignore.

Among these spaces of great architectural richness we find ovens for cooking the maguey, fermentation vats, mills, working patios, wine cellars, and *chacuacos*. This last circular element is a brick chimney of great height that contrasts with the horizontality of the rest of the buildings and is the visible reference to the location of the factory in the compound.

The ovens for cooking the maguey are constructed of stone and covered with small vaults with an opening in the top accessed by small steps. They deviate from circular or octagonal designs below the surface that appear above the surface as small cubes. In the subterranean part, there is access to a firebox to stoke the fire with the required fuel.

The mills where they crush the heart of the agave are constructed in the form of a circle enclosed by a low wall. To accomplish the milling, a team of draft animals circulated outside the circumference, causing a great millstone to rotate by means of its mechanical attachment. Mills were found under large vaulted spaces or uncovered in the work patio. Sometimes this work patio was part of the *patio de campo* or else was in a space set aside for the purpose that was delineated by the buildings of the factory. In both cases, the site contained basins and troughs where they watered the mules and oxen. The fermentation basins were rectangular and of great size and were protected by barrel vaults supported by walls and arches. Interior arches divided the space into several bays corresponding to the number of basins found in these enormous, dark, silent areas where the substance was fermented.

CHAPTER EIGHT

MATERIALS

AND

CONSTRUCTION

METHODS

CONSTRUCTION PROJECTS on the haciendas were generally linked to two principal factors: one was the economic status; the other related to the ecology of the place. The criterion of the hacienda owner to allocate the quantity of resources to a given construction was always determined by the idea of the productive enterprise that the hacienda represented. Thus, most constructions were authorized with a strict sense of economy—even to the point of having the workers construct their own houses. This contrasts with the approach to the erection of the owner's house and the chapel, for which there were no limits placed on the resources used. On occasion, spaces that stored the products that generated wealth for the hacienda were also decorated, principally on their façade, to accentuate their hierarchy within the context of the hacienda. The master plans for these edifices were often produced by professional architects.

Construction, for whatever purpose, was always related to the material resources available—resources determined by the environment of the place, by construction techniques previously used, and always in response to the prevailing climatic conditions. Construction on haciendas was an ongoing task and up to the end of the nineteenth century was characterized by a notable, and almost exclusive, utilization of local materials. The use of resources always obeys an evident logic and instinctive recognition of the best use and mechanical properties of the material.

The most important variables among the

Peñasco. Granary.

different buildings, speaking only from a construction point of view, are found in the percentage of leveled areas and in the solutions used to cover spaces. The use of leveled areas for the big house and the chapel is generally the same as for the granaries and *tinacales* when these are attached to the house. Freestanding granaries use the same in their interiors. In other constructions, leveling is used almost exclusively in areas sited near water. The difference among roofs was more significant, as some

La Ventilla.
Buttresses alongside
the granaries.

buildings were covered with flat roofs, some with cross vaults or barrel vaults, and others with less permanent slanted ones. This variety has repercussions as much in the contextual harmony as in the feeling of internal space appropriate to each habitation. We shall discuss the diverse techniques of roofing below, but for now we are concerned with the principal materials used in construction.

The existence of clays throughout the country makes them a fundamental element in construction, either raw, as in adobes, or baked, as in roofing tiles, floor tiles, or *tabiques*. Only when stone was available on a site was it used instead of adobes for erecting walls. The techniques involved in the making and use of adobe followed traditional concepts. Adobe walls were always laid on a stone foundation that was extended to form a skirt. The bricks were laid with mud mortar, and joints were chinked with diverse materials such as *tezontle*, fieldstone, fired clay, etc. For leveling surfaces, a mortar was made whose principal ingredient was powdered lime. Protection of adobe walls in their corners, doors, and windows was also accomplished by traditional means with reinforcements of *tabique*, fieldstone, or cut stone. The latter was carved or polished, depending upon the importance of the opening, and was used in combination with wood as jambs for doors and gates and frequently as horizontal reinforcements for apertures or in the culmination of walls under the mezzanine or terrace roof in order to distribute the weight uniformly on the adobe wall. Owing to the self-sufficient character of the hacienda

Pozo del Carmen. New house. Entry portal.

and the availability of numerous artisans, clays could be transformed into a diversity of fired pieces, from the common *tabique* to specially designed elements. The criteria used in this production were the following: bricks measured 2.5 × 15 × 28 cm; floor tiles from 2.5 × 20 × 20 cm to 2.5 × 30 × 30 cm. Other dimensions were employed for interior and exterior floors and in the construction of flat arches formed of brick. Brick was also used, in combination with other pieces in the form of half circles, to form handrails and lattice windows. *Tabique* was principally used as a reinforcing material in adobe walls or in combination with stone in rubble-stone walls. Only at the end of the nineteenth century was it used in the manner apparent on the façades of big houses, as in the cases of San Lorenzo, Chimalpa, and San Francisco Soltepec, where it was incorporated as decorative detail into cornices, balconies, pediments, and other elements. There is another type of *tabique*, smaller in size, that was used in the construction of vaults.

The erection of walls on a stone foundation depended upon the existence of an abundance of stone at the location of the compound, as in the case of San Pedro Tochatlaco. Stone was used in its natural state, set with mortar in most cases, and chinked with small stones. In the building of low walls, stones were set without mortar in some cases. These were lightly worked to attain a better fit in the wall. Low walls still enclosing the ruins of many haciendas testify to the durability of this technique.

An important environmental factor that directly impacts modes of construction, most significantly of roofs, is the existence of forests. Wood is used in practically all constructions, since its ability to bear stress and compression makes it particularly versatile. Its use ranges from roof beams, to shingles, to supporting columns—even those of great height, as in the granaries of Segura in Tlaxcala. Timbers of

smaller diameter are used at less cost in inclined roofs; as planks for doors, gates, and windows; as floorboards; as gears for waterwheels; as supports for the vats used in the fermentation of pulque; as arms in the mescal mills, and in the endless quantity of furniture and implements pertinent to the production of the farm.

The absence of appropriate wood in the area of some haciendas of San Luis Potosí encouraged the development of arches. This technique is the most advanced that was used in hacienda construction, since it is a specialty that not all master builders were able to achieve. In the haciendas of Tlaxcala and Hidalgo, it was used almost exclusively in chapels and sporadically in some *tinacales* or granaries that date from the same period of construction as the chapels. In the state of San Luis Potosí, there are buildings, as at Peotillos, where the covered spaces are achieved with vaults, while in other places in the same region they reached a solution by using clay jars mortared together in the manner of caissons.

Other methods of roofing using wood include the flat wooden roof covered with a brick vault or with shingles or earth, and the sloped roof made with wood beams—as on some granaries—which support a wooden deck made of planks covered with tiles, or else logs and lath sheeting that directly support the tile, such as those used on mule pens and workers' quarters. The number of sloping roofs in these constructions varies according to the placement of the buildings within the compound: when they are attached to a wall, they use a slope toward the opposite side; if freestanding, as in the case of some workers' quarters, the roofs will have two or three slopes, depending upon the formal intentions.

The shedding of rainwater from flat or vaulted roofs is accomplished in two ways: one by means of gargoyles and the other by means of either open or covered ducts embedded in the walls. Independent of their function, these solutions acquire formal importance by their location on the façades, becoming in many examples a very important composition element through their rhythmic treatment and through the colors and textures that developed over time.

Another important element within the construction process is supports, such as columns or pilasters and arches or lintels. Traditional materials such as fieldstone, *tabique*, adobe, and cut stone were used in their fabrication. This type of solution was employed in main entry porticos as well as in those of the patio of the big house and at the center of spaces requiring big spans, as in the case of granaries, *tinacales*, or mescal works. Because of its quality, cut stone was the preferred material for columns and arches in the big house, whereas other materials were used for the remaining buildings. The solution for load-bearing elements with arches used in haciendas offers a lesson in the utilization of the material applied with two opposing methodologies: the popular and the academic.

The academic applies laws of composition pertaining to cut stone whose designs are well proportioned when executed by professionals. But when these elements follow the caprice of the owner, through the eclectic trend that arose at the end of the nineteenth century, they lose, in addition to their proportions, all seriousness and remain as nothing more than superfluous ornament. In contrast to the latter are popular solutions that work with local materials. These solutions arose out of the logical handling of the tectonic nature of the material. The adobe arches of the cowsheds of Ciénega de Mata and the interior arcades in the ruins of the granary of Cuamantzingo celebrate the arch with integral arrangements. The development of the arch depends upon the natural context: it is used less when there is sufficient wood.

Cast iron is a material introduced to haciendas at the end of the nineteenth century and is used in supporting elements. Thus, in this epoch, traditional materials are replaced by these slim and graceful prefabricated columns. Steel technology turns up in the small girders used as beams in flat roofs and as roof finishings for openings.

Construction methods on haciendas incorporate important aspects, methods, and materials of the era that transformed architecture. This attitude toward changing construction methods is a lesson that we should keep in mind today as we consider our methods and requirements, which now are infinitely more extensive, and make our choices much more difficult.

CHAPTER NINE

CONSIDERING

DETAILS

ABOVE AND BELOW, within and without, to the last corner of the hacienda, we encounter details—elements that reinforce our proposition that the life of the hacienda can be understood through its architecture. Throughout our work, we have mentioned many details to focus on some whole. Now we propose to separate them from the rest and examine them individually, but even from this more limited and focused perspective, one observes the same qualities that we have pointed out in speaking of the whole.

The aesthetic intent is also quite evident in the details, and in some examples it derives from current fashion, from academic standards, or from the wealth or caprice of the proprietor, while in other examples, its origin is found in popular inspiration. The social hierarchy, requirements of labor, housing, recreation, and religion are manifested in the quantity, form, composition, and location of the details.

OPENINGS AND CLOSINGS

Interiors and exteriors, the inside and the outside are linked by openings. As a whole, these elements are subordinate to the wall, and their vertical presence in individual examples contributes to the horizontality of the façades. The number of doors and windows, their repetition, rhythm, form, and size—be they interior or exterior, principal or secondary— give directional flow to the façades.

The function of doors is to connect one space with another; that of windows is to illuminate and give warmth to the rooms. Apart

Tepenacasco. Openings in the finial of the zaguán.

Peñasco. Opening on the side of a ramp.

San Pedro Tochatlaco.

Tecomalucan.

San Martín Notario.

Mal País.

Tlalayote.

Tepetates.

from the functional aspect of openings, they are apt to be accompanied by other intentions: such would appear to be the case where a door or window serves as a pretext to manifest religious reverence, the opulence of the owners, or a preoccupation with the symmetry of the whole. In extreme cases, we find unnecessary or imitation doors and windows, and openings whose size and richness surpass their function or fulfill it only with great difficulty. By way of contrast, doors in the workers' quarters were so insubstantial that the workers who inhabited them had to resort to curtains to achieve a modicum of protection and privacy.

In regard to their form, windows open like the flared bell of a horn to the interior space, after passing through thick walls. The final extent of the angle allows for the erection of benches on the sides without blocking the passage of light and warmth. Most windows are rectangular or square and never too big. Some are vertical, narrow openings like loopholes, others rounded like oculi or finished off with an arch or oval. They never have glass panes and are frequently completed with hoods, shutters, and wooden grills. Chapel windows made of delicate sheets of onyx—that Mexican alabaster worked so well by our stonecutters—give hue to the light. There are windows so small that they only admit a ray of light and others that just serve as a delicate accent over a door.

But windows were not the only elements utilized as accents for doors: niches; lintels; shell shapes; and frames of plaster, cut stone, or brick made them stand out, along with the

Noria de Gámez.   TOP: *Tecajete.*   *Noria la Tapona.*

La Noria.

beautiful work in wood and wrought iron that emphasized important doors in chapels and the big house in the *patio de campo*. More functional are those doors without surprises or disruptions that access aligned rooms.

BETWEEN HEAVEN AND EARTH

Between heaven and earth are staircases: formal and service, interior and exterior, of field or cut stone, tiled or whitewashed. They are always attached to or enclosed by walls, with the notable exceptions of Gogorrón and San Martín Notario, whose formal stairways inside the big house are detached and bifurcated, ascending on two sides from a common landing in imperial style. The forms and styles of stairways are closely linked to their location. Those that access the bell tower or choir loft of chapels, for example, are spiraled or spindled[1] and contained within a cylindrical or cubic space, while those at San Gil are built into polygonal spaces that climb to belvederes.

Staircases that connect the lower story with the rooms of the upper floor in the big house tend to be one uninterrupted flight of steps, as seen in Totoapa or Mazaquiahuac. This simple design with only one landing can be even more elemental, as in the astonishing interior ramp we encounter in La Ventilla. This zigzag ramp and its complicated design prompt many hypotheses, but here we simply note its existence and repeat the popular explanation that we collected in our fieldwork: "This ramp allowed mules burdened with gold to ascend to the rooms where the owner's fortune was kept."

Exterior staircases also exhibit more or less sophistication in accordance with their location and the purpose they serve. In Tetlapaya, for example, a double central stairway solves the problem of the unevenness of the patio and creates a vertical plane that deftly accommodates a fountain. In Pozo del Carmen, a very long stairway zigzags across the mountainous terrain that separates two areas of construction. Silhouetting their austere profile against the sky, simple stairs climb to service patios, wells, terraces, granaries, mescal ovens, and barrel vaults. Inside the houses, balustrades and handrails of forged iron or turned wood protect the owners with a certain elegance. But, with these exceptions, hacienda staircases are constructed with no urge to pretentiousness. Between heaven and earth, compositions of great sculptural effect, whose richness consists in the equilibrium, harmony, rhythm, and economy with which the elements are combined, are put together with a natural flair.

Staircases govern the play between vertical and horizontal planes by extending or penetrating volumes and by integrating them, without railings or balustrades, to the different levels and walls. In this manner, landings, lintels, walls, floors, arches, and corridors are blended with stair treads, elevations, and profiles.

CONCLUDING DETAILS

Finally, to conclude the discussion of details we must point out the role that texture and color play in the spaces of the hacienda. This interplay of severe contrasting elements does nothing

Tecoac. Trough.

Recoba. Gargoyle.

more than repeat the audacious use of diverse colors and textures in other architectural spaces of our country. Polished walls occur against cut-stone frames; blue walls appear next to the burnished red of a clay floor. Colors and textures playing in each space the game with the sun that is so typical of these Mexican latitudes.

Details are resolved in a unique way with intuitive solutions that reflect the cultural identity of their creators. The power of this feeling is such that it allows us to recognize, even in the details, the origin and raison d'être of this architecture. With the full strength of their originality, details contribute to the whole to complete the creative work—always unique and unrepeatable—that we are able to study in each hacienda.

Ciénega de Mata.
Portal of the main patio.

CHAPTER TEN

CONCLUSION

It is easy for the reader to have
forgotten that which he knew,
that while systems, schools,
and theories come and go,
the sediment of eternal truths,
of the eternal essence,
continues to take shape.

MIGUEL DE UNAMUNO

THROUGHOUT THE DRAWINGS and images of this work we have sought to uncover the fundamental architectural principles of haciendas, enveloping them in the spatial environments that we feel are integral to the magic of this architecture. We have spoken of unvarying elements—constants that originated in concepts derived from ways of life that remain almost unchanged during four centuries in our country. We found through our investigation that this phenomenon is an important marker in the development of the organization and the forms typical of Mexican architecture.

It was no surprise that the organization and forms of hacienda architecture should be the same as those in the rest of Hispanic-American architecture: "horizontality, organization of volumes around an uncovered space (patio), use of materials according to their inherent building properties, dominance of the wall over the opening, decorative accumulation on some façades that contrasts with the simplicity of the others"[1]—concepts that corroborate the homogeneous attitude of a cultural entity without losing the imagination and regional and individual fantasy.

In this architectural universe, we find criteria that suggest the methods to pursue to produce an architecture of our time that arises from its land—this is to say, with a national identity. In the haciendas, the sensitive observer can find diverse elements capable of leading to untapped, contemporaneous solutions. One can also find modern values, speaking in a merely architectural sense, that invite us to

reflect and go deeper into our history to search for the expression of our own time.

For us, haciendas are not just historic buildings. Nor do we seek to re-create them in new constructions, like the revivals of the nineteenth century. We simply reflect on the modern values suggested by this architecture, which are not so easy to analyze and which— if one endeavors to reuse diverse concepts and elements—require one to look for the strict local reasons dictated by the physical environment (local materials, climate, light, winds) and the geographic, social, and historical influences that produced them, provided that there is justification for their use in our time.

Another issue raised by this phenomenon is the attitude that prevails in the architecture of religion and power (wealth) in the nineteenth century. The use of borrowed architectural styles produced truly awkward eclecticisms, sometimes to the extreme of caricaturization. Such examples recall the attitudes that tried to disassociate themselves from their land, their history, and their culture. In spite of this, haciendas still evince the constants that make up the principal characteristic of this architectural endeavor. Thus, just as the monastic architecture of the sixteenth century contributed the atrium, the *posa chapels*, the *open chapel*, and other elements, the hacienda brought forth the *tinacal* as another gift of Mexican architecture to the world. This element was undervalued at the time when resources were committed to its construction. It is precisely in the second half of the nineteenth century and the beginning of the twentieth that the cold stylistic aspirations of the proprietors often resulted in neoclassic, neo-Gothic, or neo-Arabic styles that curtailed the warm, popular building traditions.

Visiting these buildings, immersing ourselves in their environments, has had a great impact on our views as architects. We have found a source that has resonated in an important way on our professional work. Mystery, surprise, and memory will tend to be reflected in our work through our cultural baggage, which, after this study, reaffirms our faith in the cultural identity of our country, which has already had in this and other arts first-rate exponents. Barragán, Rivera, and Rulfo[2] are examples of guides to follow in pursuit of our fulfillment in spaces and poetic environments that emanate from within. We hope that this work may stimulate other similar interests that will deepen our understanding of these architectural phenomena in order to participate in the universal currents through our cultural identity.

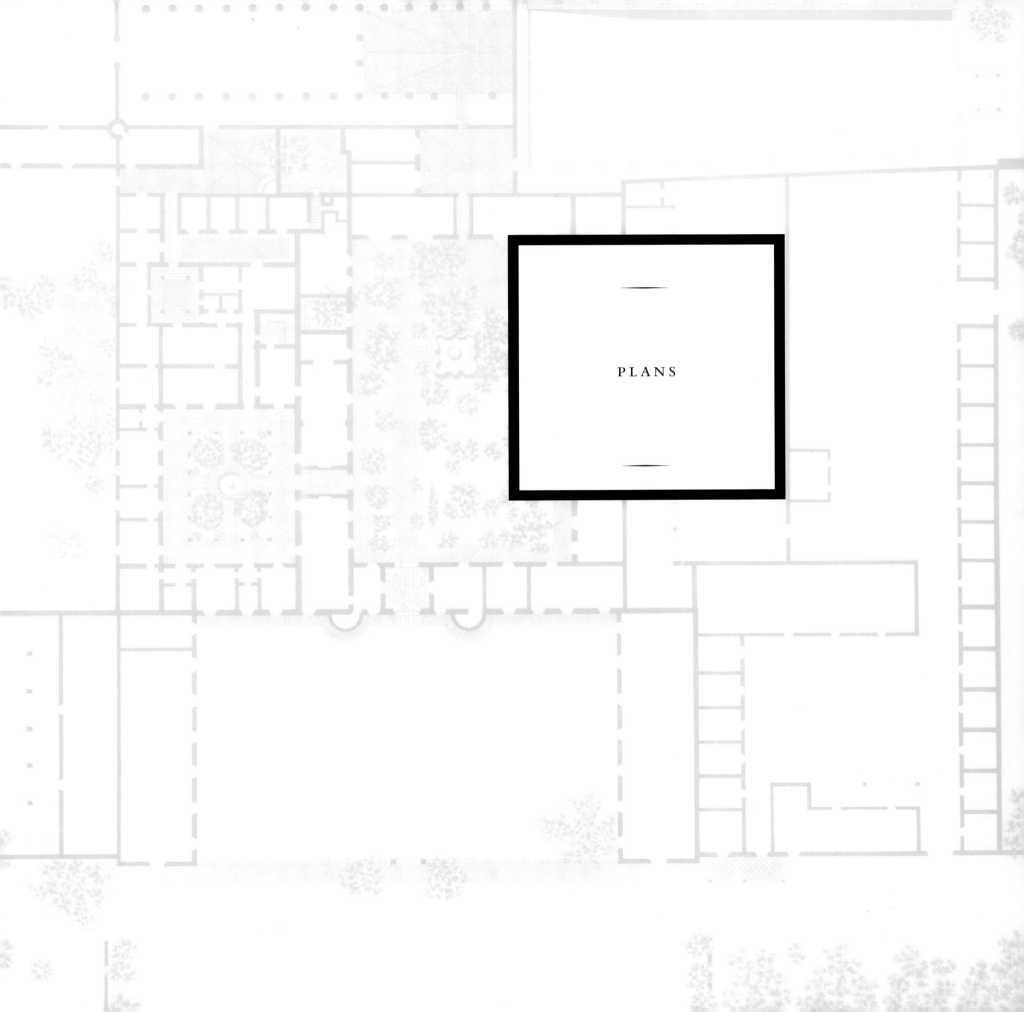

PLANS

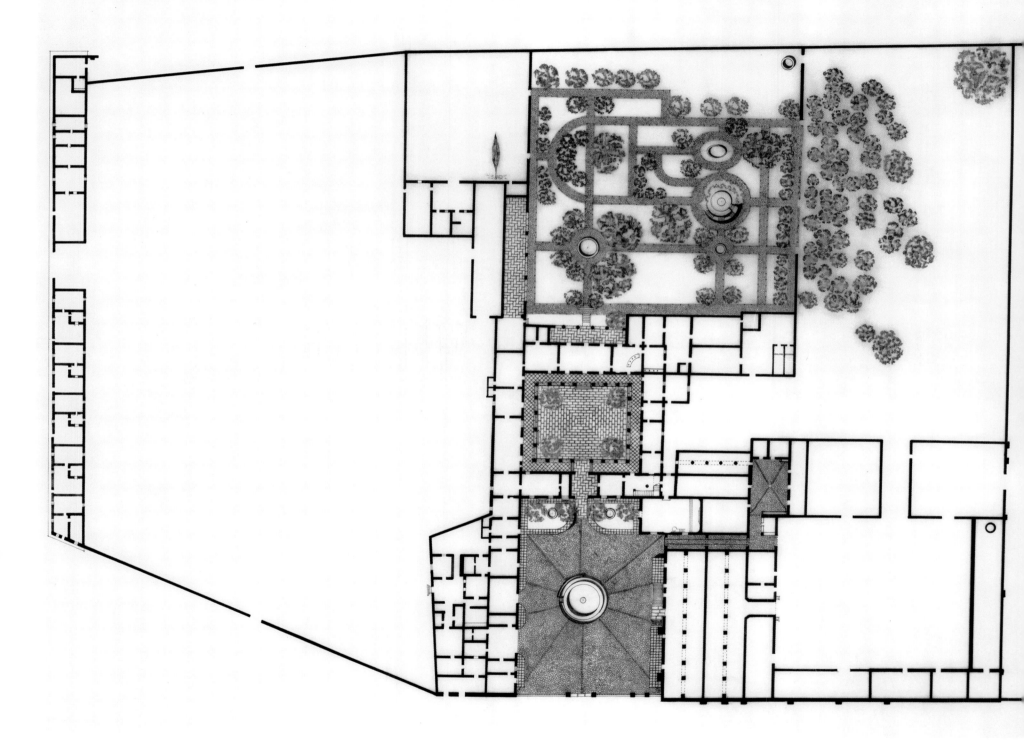

OCOTEPEC

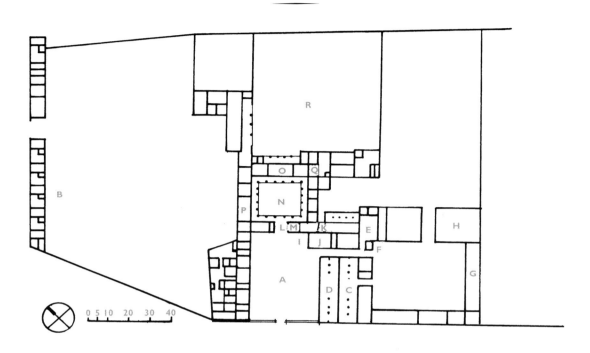

A	Patio de campo	**J**	*Chapel*
B	*Workers' quarters*	**K**	*Sacristy*
C	*Granary*	**L**	Zaguán
D	Tinacal	**M**	*Office*
E	*Stables*	**N**	*Patio*
F	*Tack room*	**O**	*Dining room*
G	*Cow Shed*	**P**	*Habitation*
H	*Corral*	**Q**	*Kitchen*
I	*Atrium*	**R**	*Orchard or garden*

CUAMANTZINGO

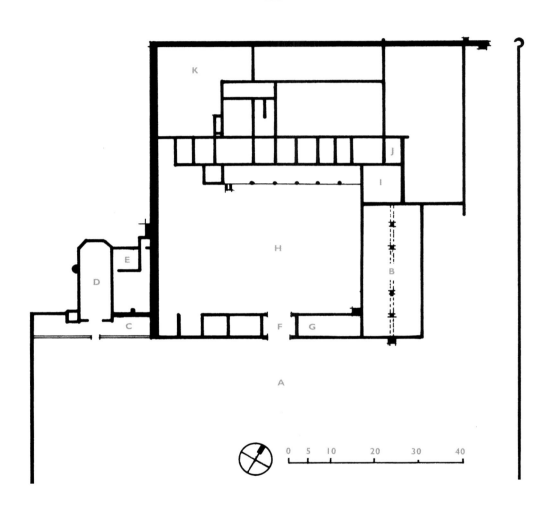

0 5 10   20   30   40

A Patio de campo   G *Office*

B *Granary*   H *Patio*

C *Atrium*   I *Dining room*

D *Chapel*   J *Kitchen*

E *Sacristy*   K *Orchard or garden*

F Zaguán

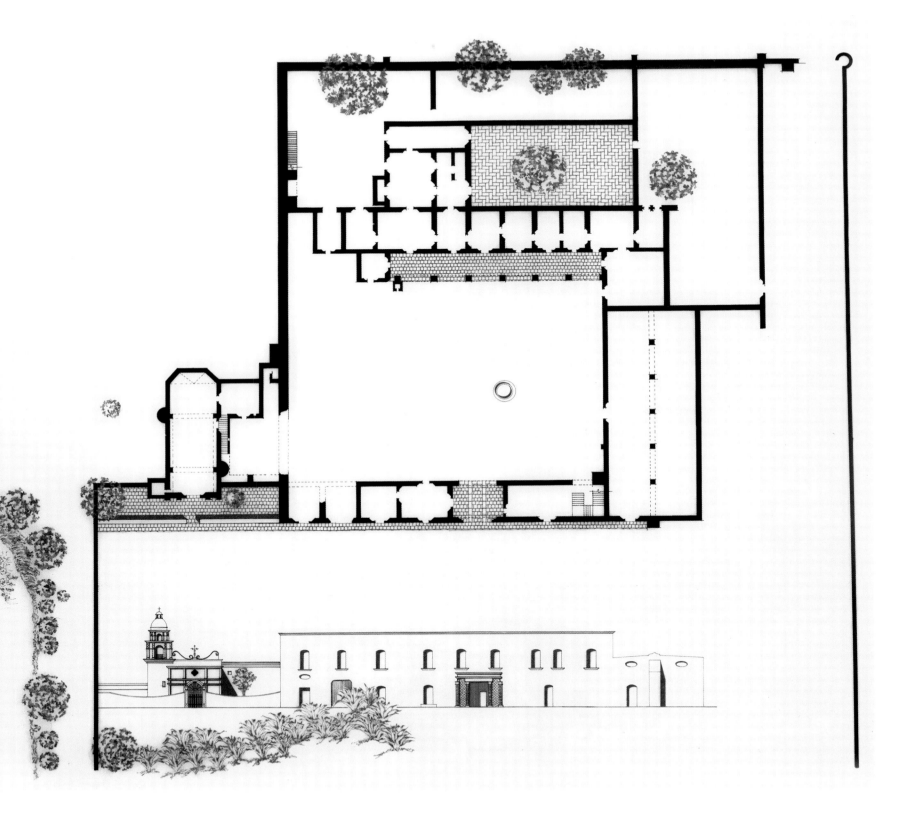

TECAJETE

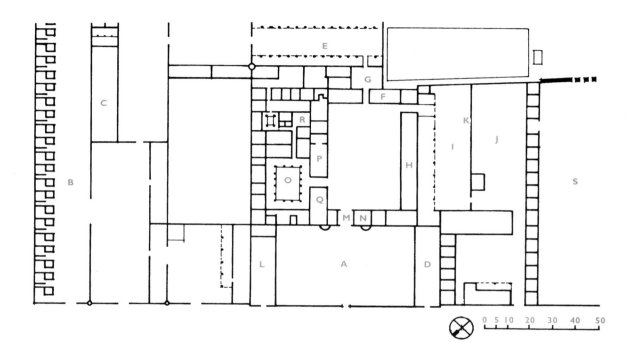

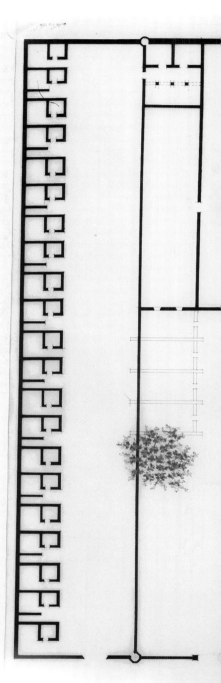

A Patio de campo	**K** *Drinking trough*
B *Workers' quarters*	**L** *Chapel*
C *Granary*	**M** Zaguán
D Tinacal	**N** *Office*
E *Stables*	**O** *Patio*
F *Coach house*	**P** *Dining room*
G *Tack room*	**Q** *Living room*
H *Cow shed*	**R** *Kitchen*
I *Mule pen*	**S** *Orchard or garden*
J *Corral*	

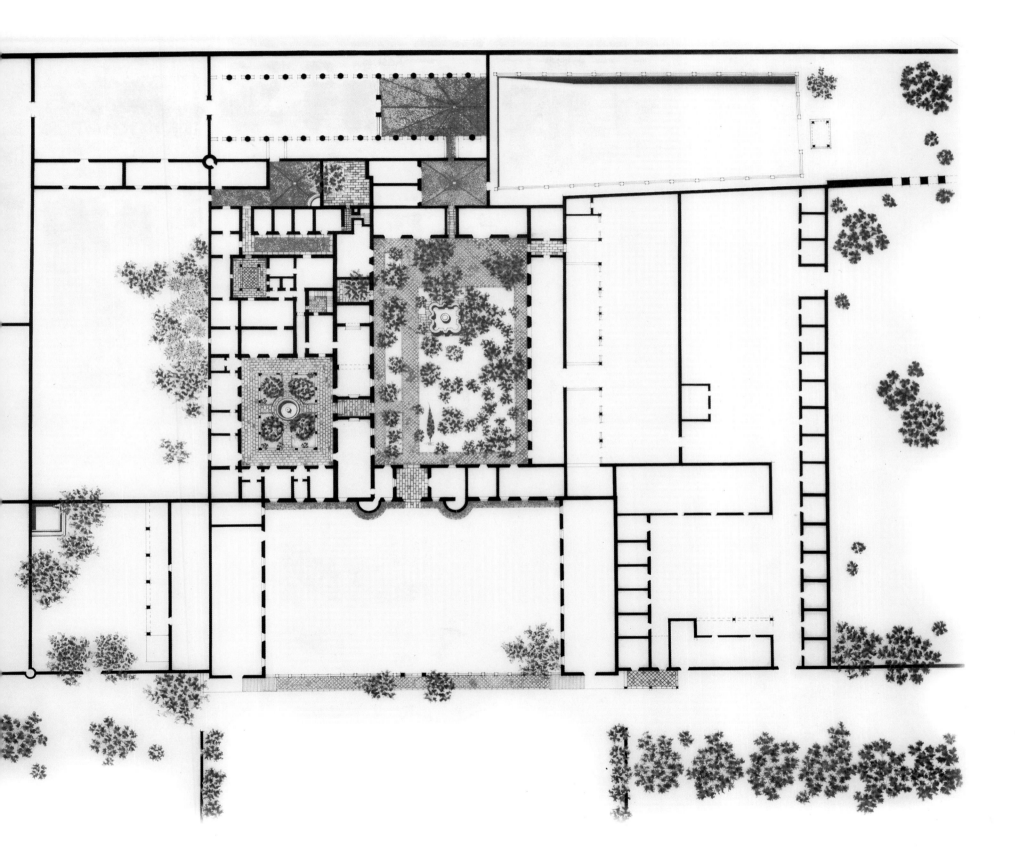

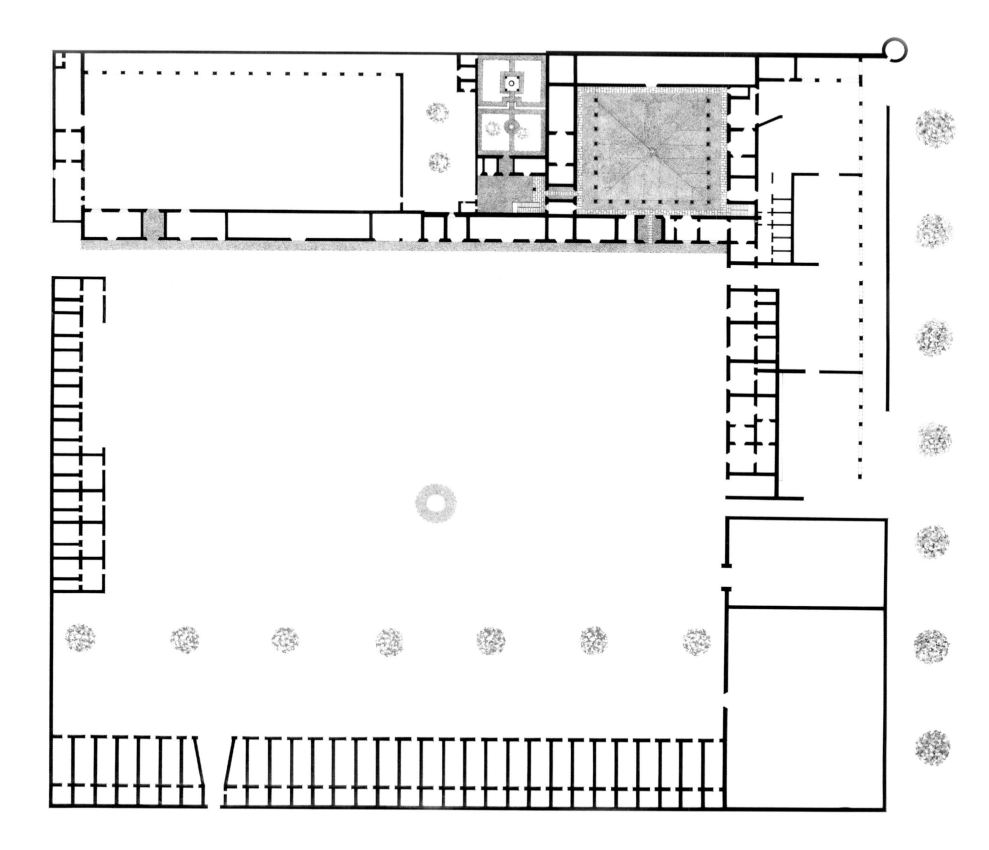

TEPALCA

FIRST LEVEL

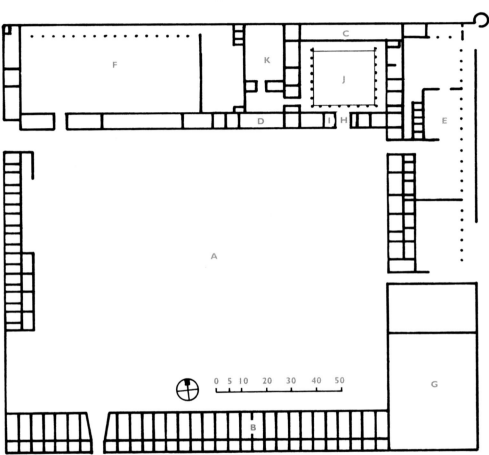

A Patio de campo
B *Workers' quarters*
C *Granary*
D Tinacal
E *Stables*
F *Cow shed*

G *Corral*
H Zaguán
I *Office*
J *Patio*
K *Orchard or garden*

TEPALCA

SECOND LEVEL

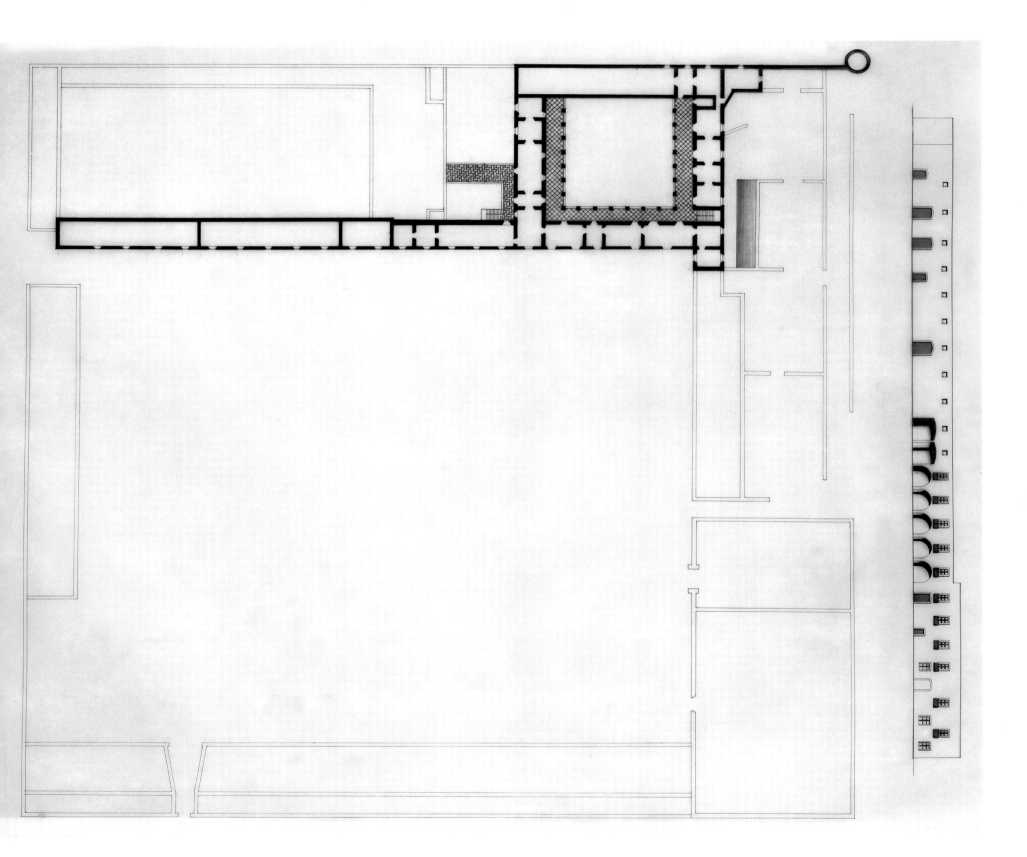

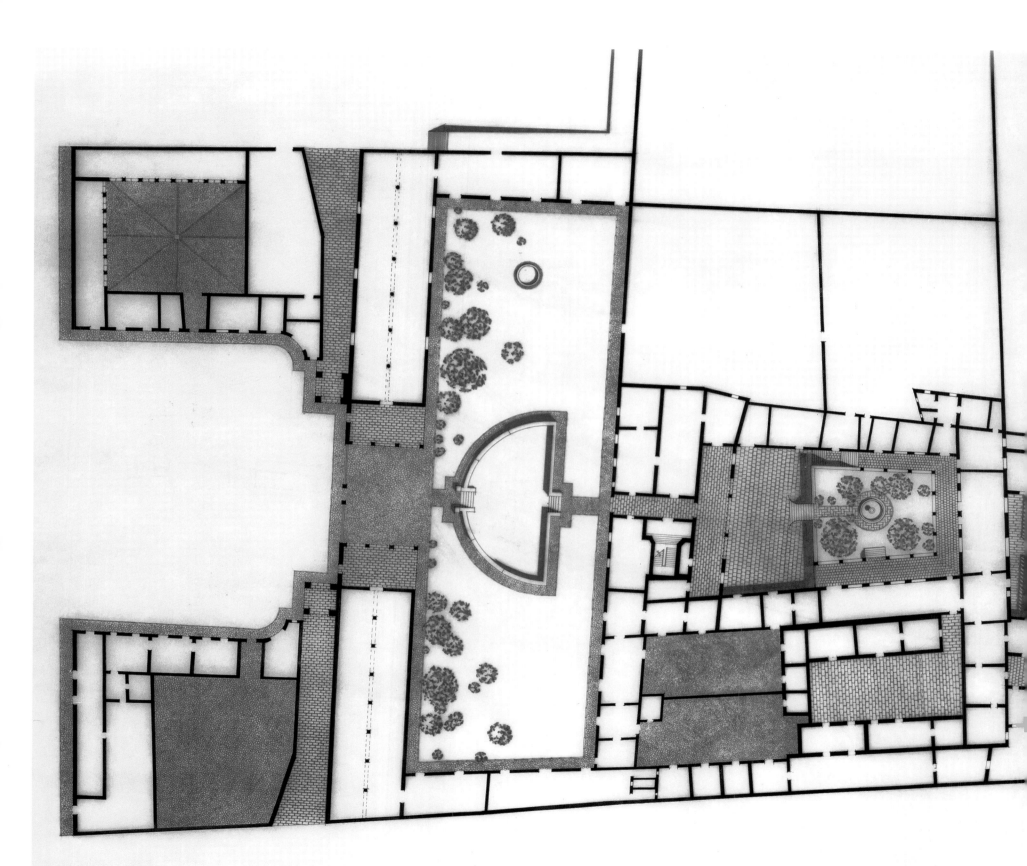

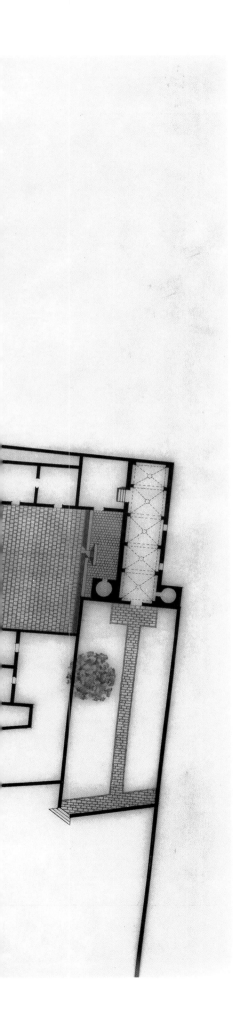

FIRST LEVEL

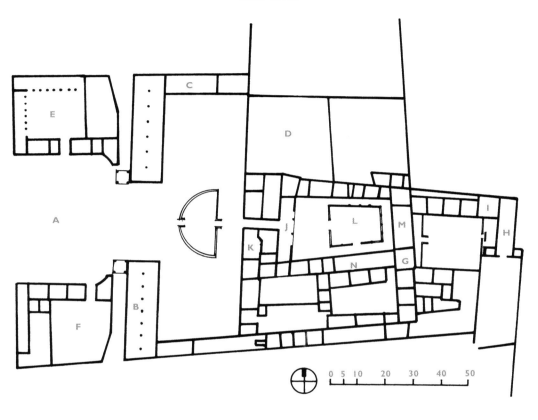

A Patio de campo		**H** *Chapel*	
B *Granary*		**I** *Sacristy*	
C Tinacal		**J** Zaguán	
D *Stables*		**K** *Office*	
E *Cow shed*		**L** *Patio*	
F *Corral*		**M** *Dining room*	
G *Kitchen*		**N** *Living room*	

MAZAQUIAHUAC

SECOND LEVEL

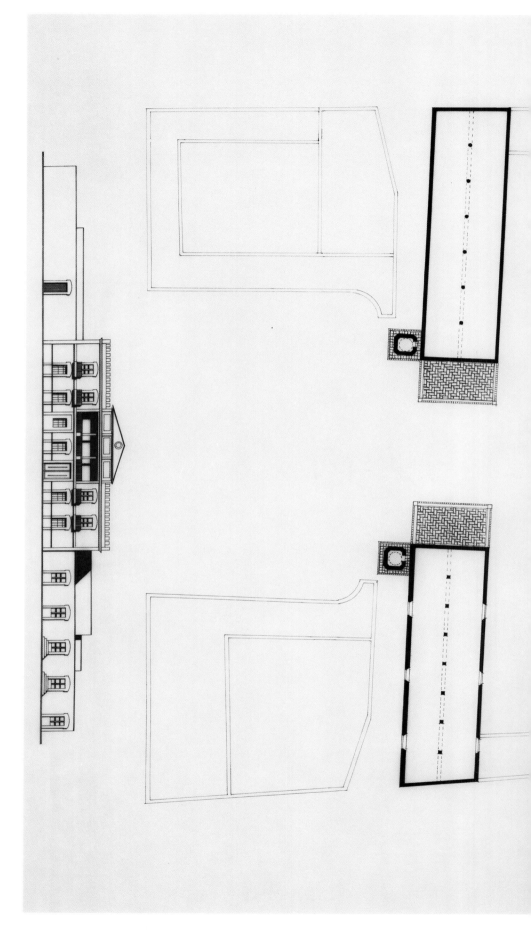

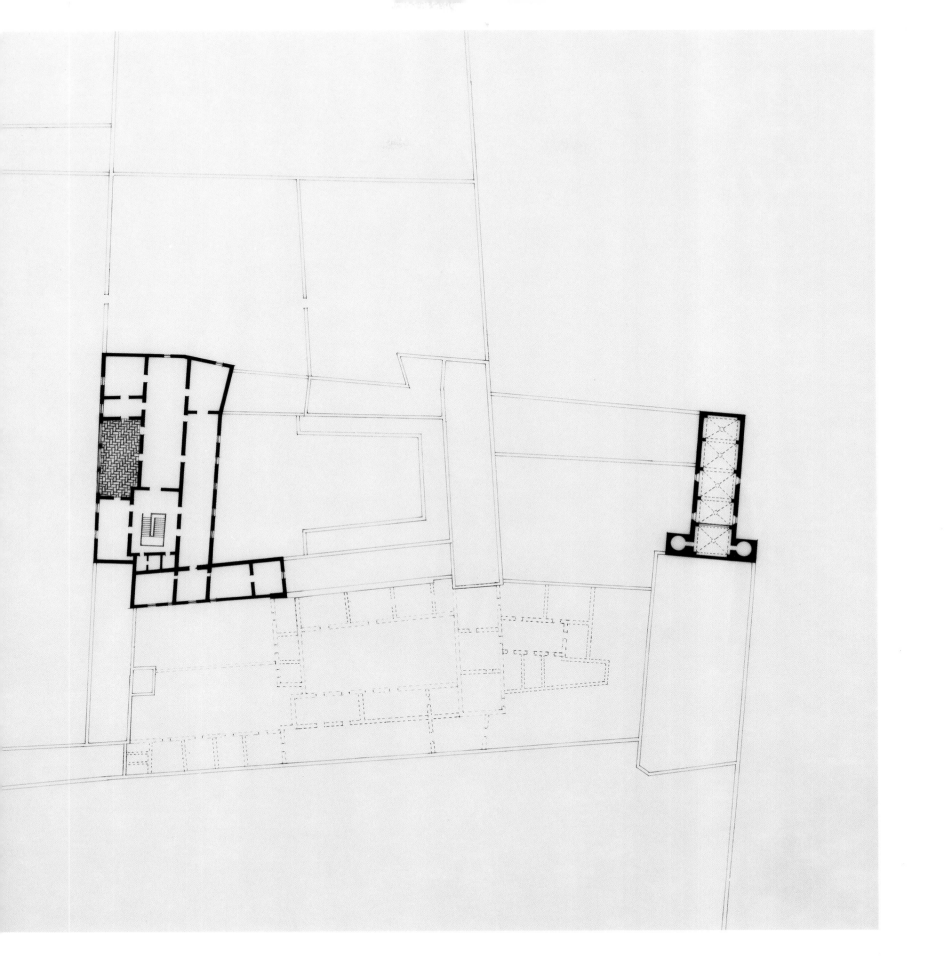

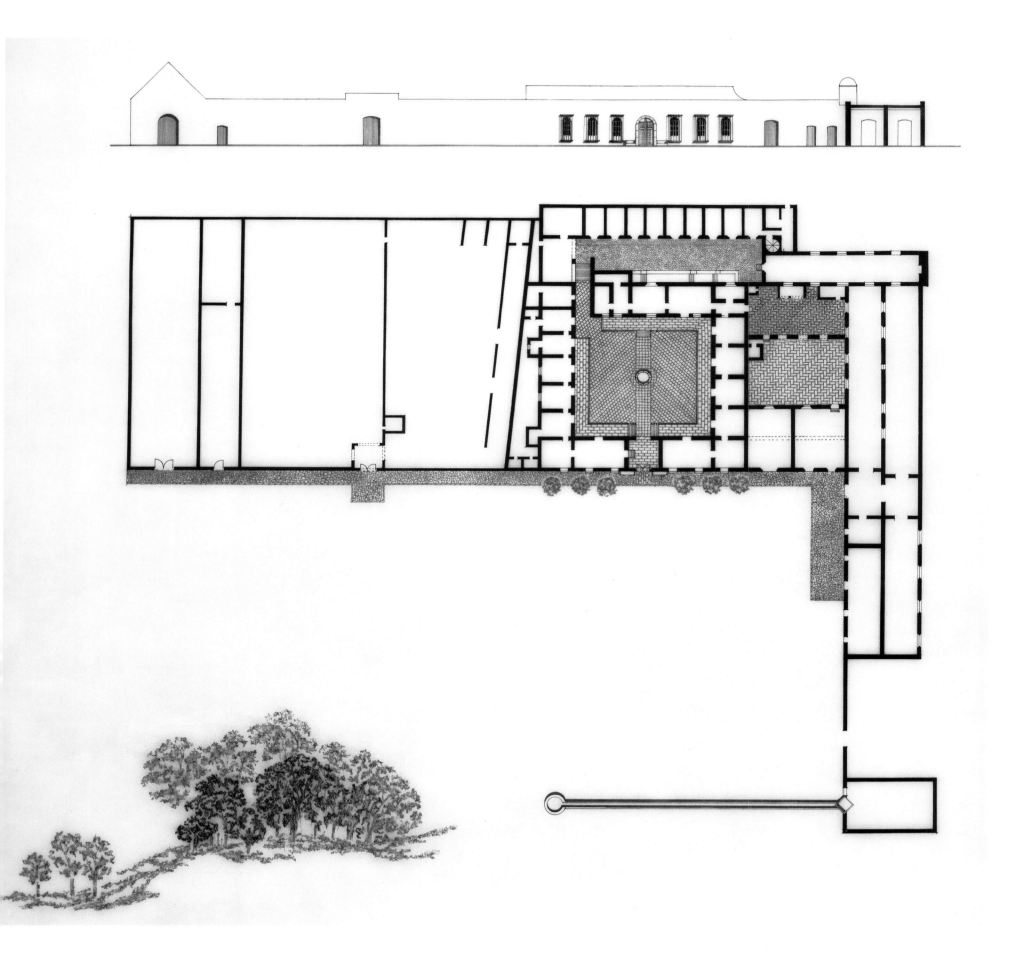

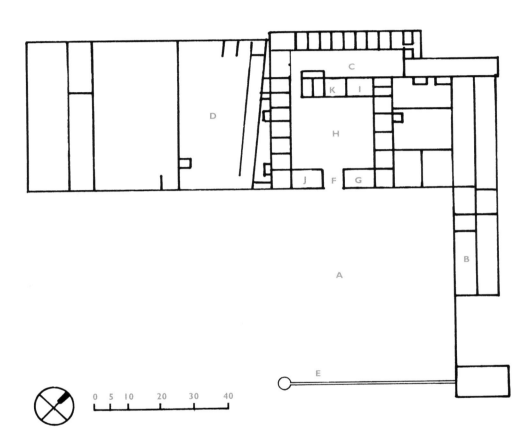

0 5 10   20   30   40

A Patio de campo   G *Office*

B *Granary*   H *Patio*

C *Stables*   I *Dining room*

D *Corral*   J *Living room*

E *Drinking trough*   K *Kitchen*

F Zaguán

LA VENTILLA

FIRST LEVEL

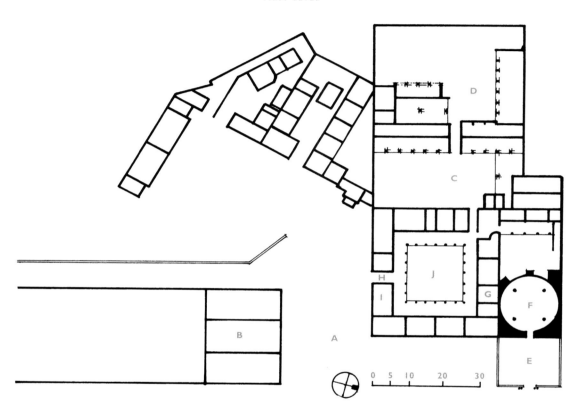

0 5 10   20   30

A Patio de campo   F Chapel
B Granary   G Sacristy
C Stables   H Zaguán
D Cow shed   I Office
E Atrium   J Patio

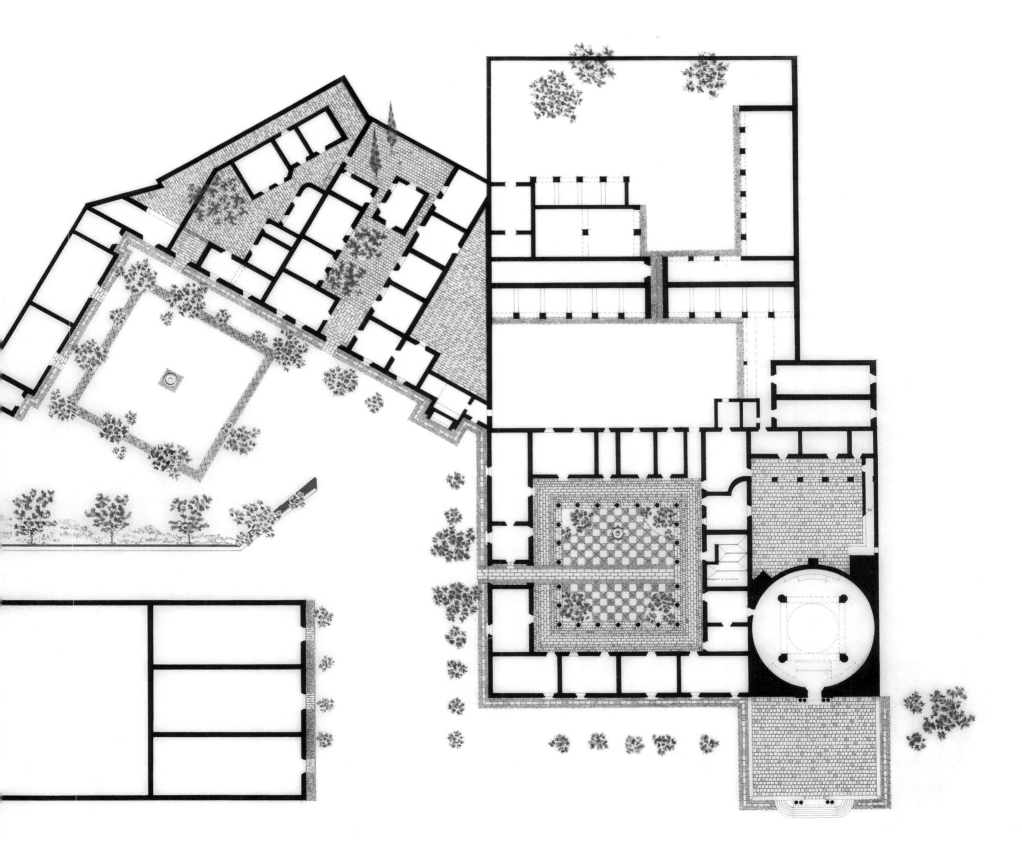

LA VENTILLA

SECOND LEVEL

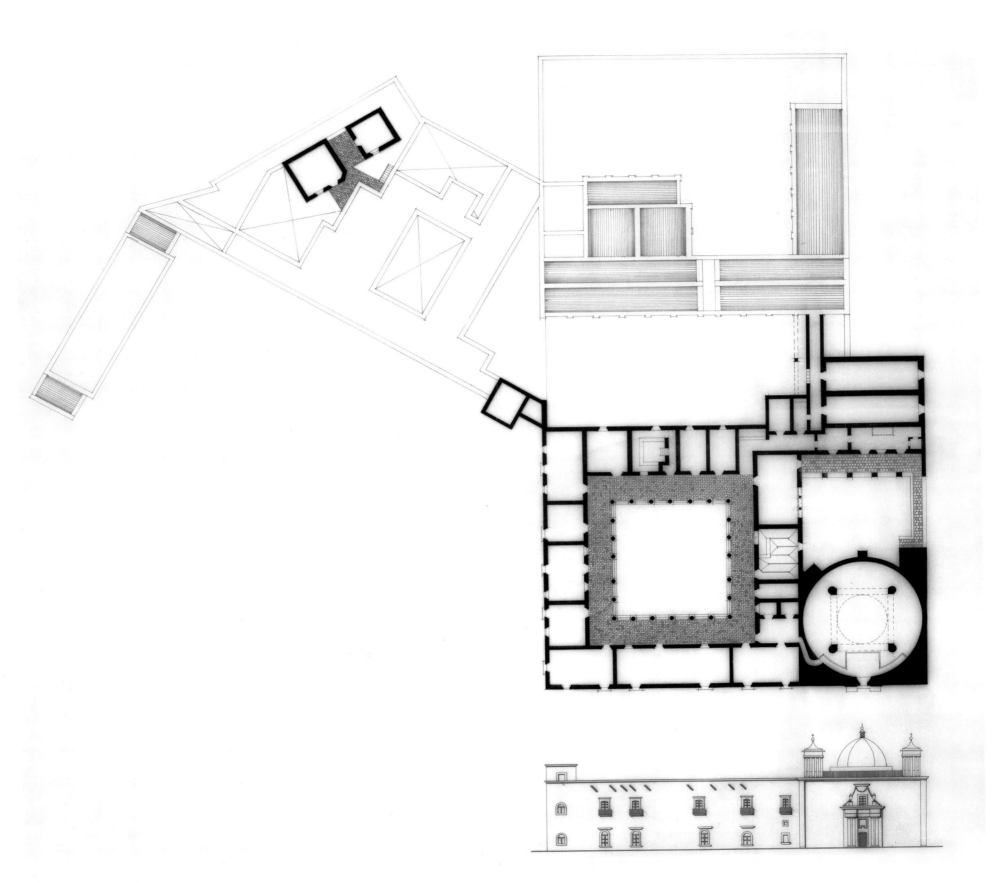

TETLAPAYA

FIRST LEVEL

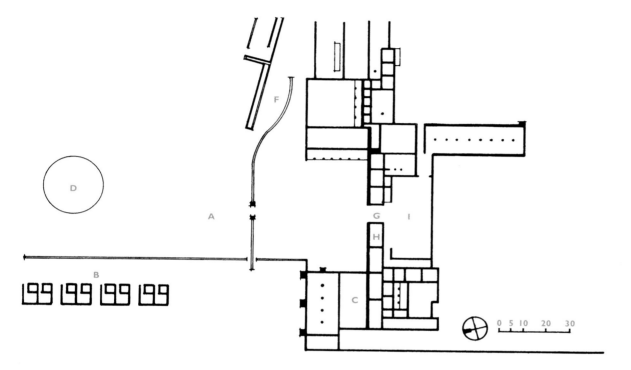

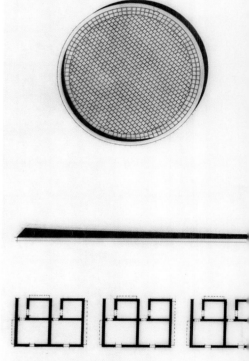

A Patio de campo   F *Watering trough*
B *Workers' quarters*   G Zaguán
C *Granary*   H *Office*
D *Threshing floor*   I *Patio*
E Tinacal

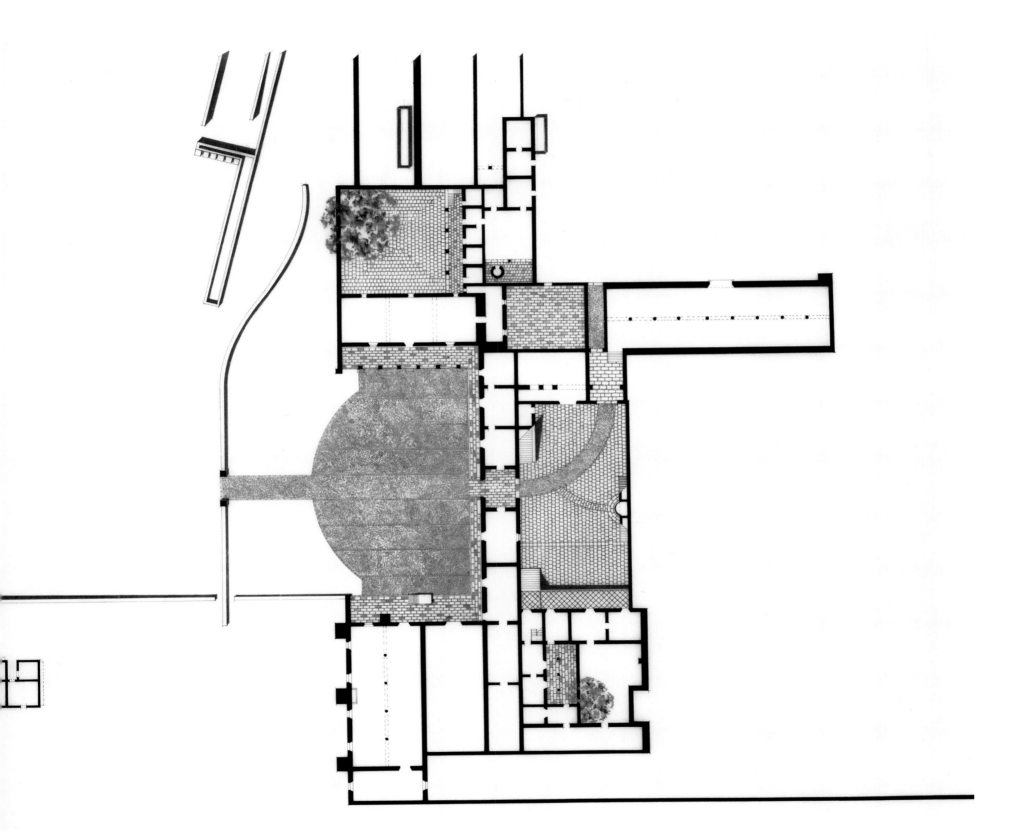

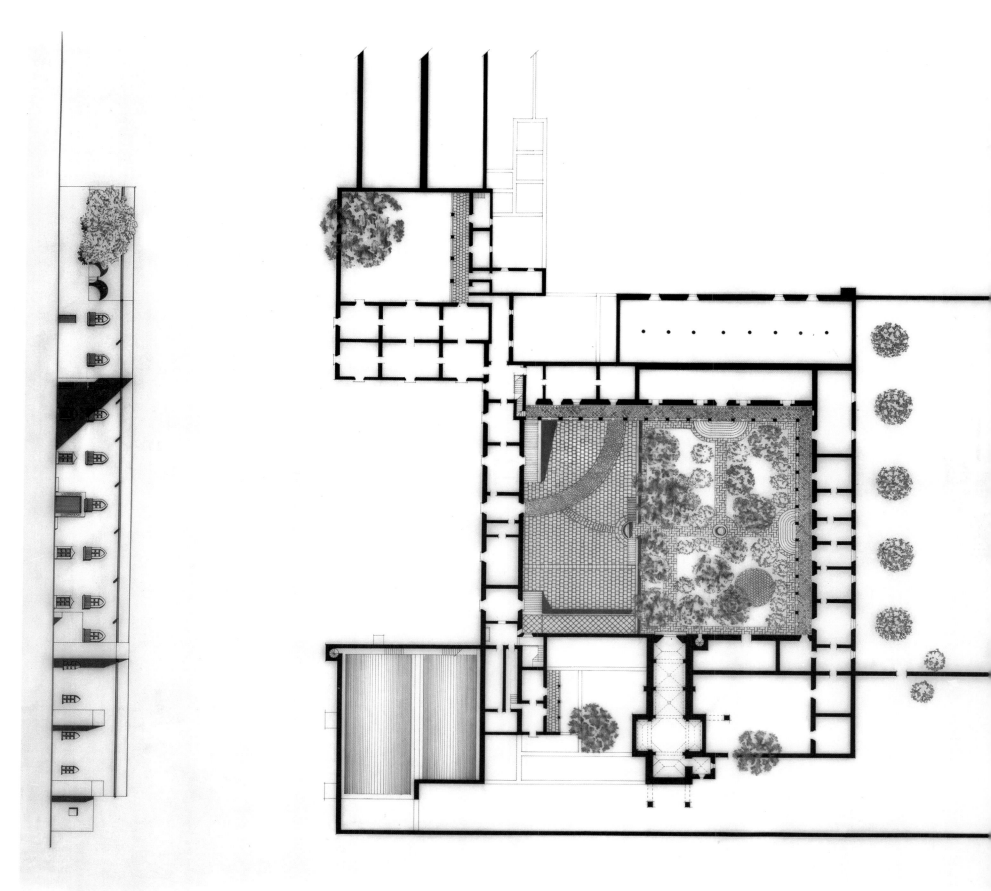

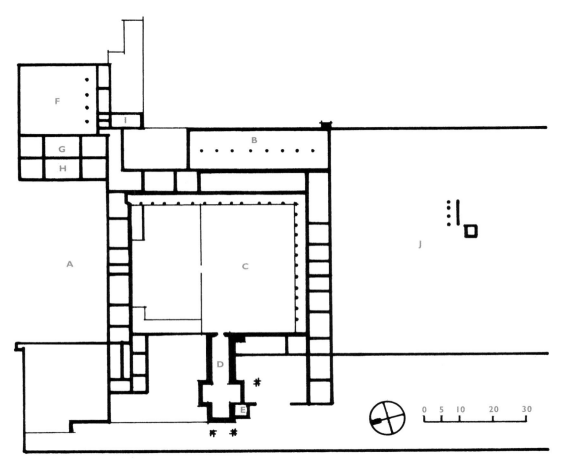

TETLAPAYA

SECOND LEVEL

A Patio de campo F Patio

B Granary G Dining room

C Atrium H Living room

D Chapel I Kitchen

E Sacristy J Orchard or garden

GOGORRÓN

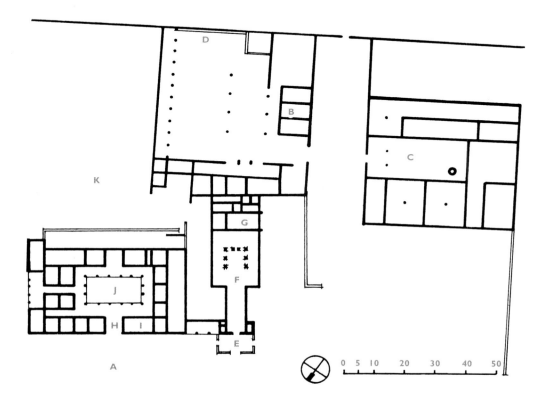

A Patio de campo G Sacristy

B Granary H Zaguán

C Mescal works I Office

D Watering trough J Patio

E Atrium K Orchard or garden

F Chapel

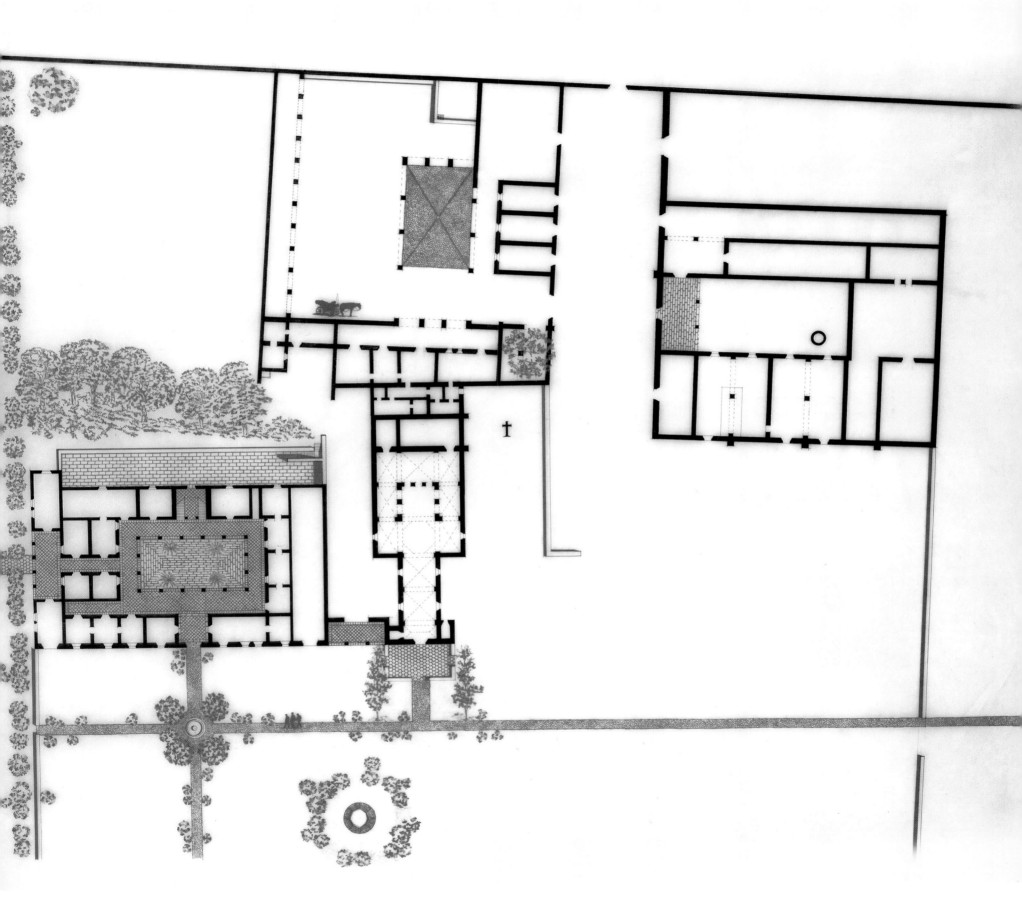

GOGORRÓN

SECOND LEVEL

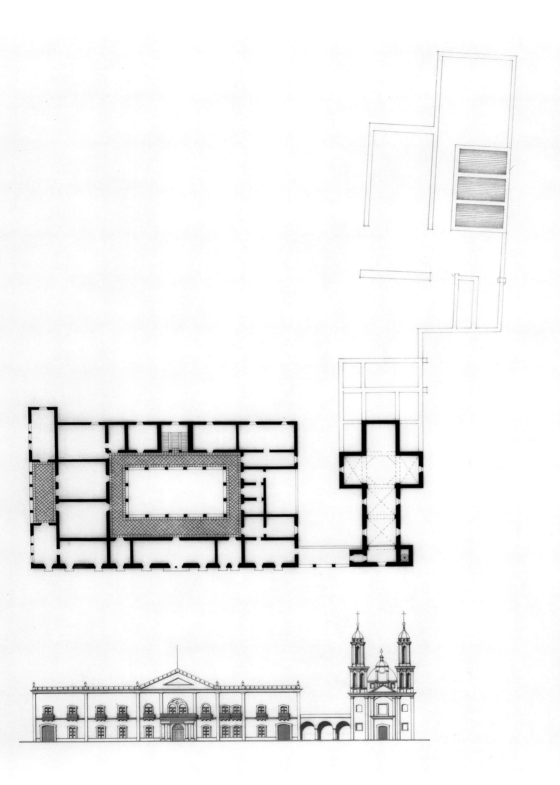
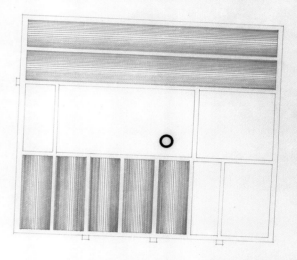

XALPATLAHUAYA

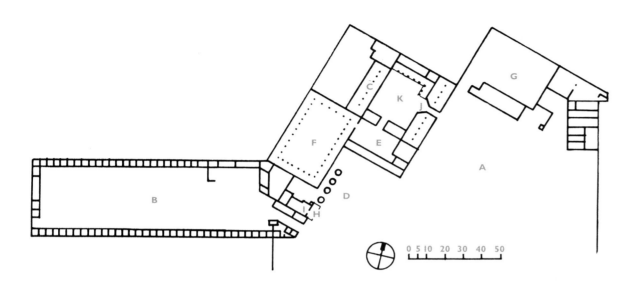

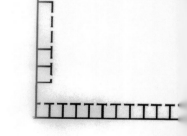

A Patio de campo   G *Corral*
B *Workers' quarters* H *Atrium*
C *Granary*   I *Chapel*
D *Silo*   J *Zaguán*
E *Stables*   K *Patio*
F *Mule pen*

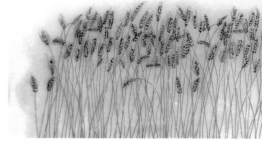

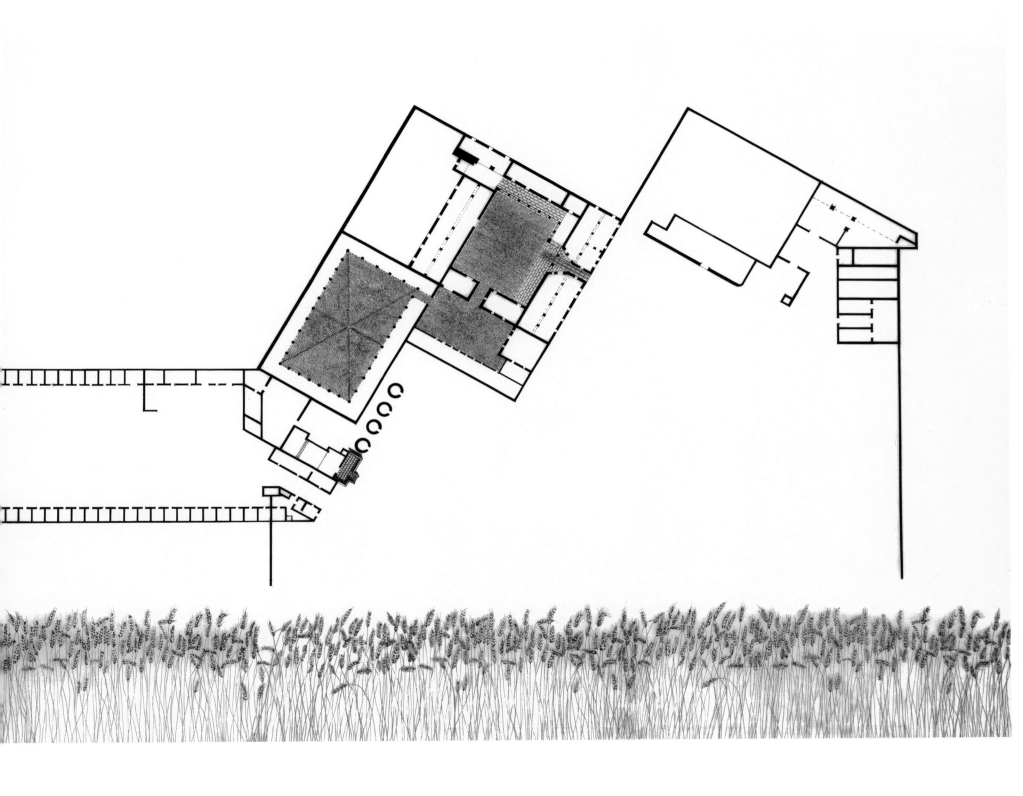

SAN FRANCISCO SOLTEPEC

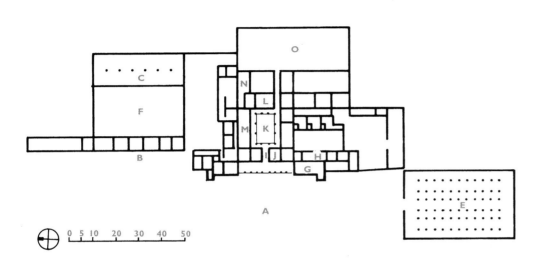

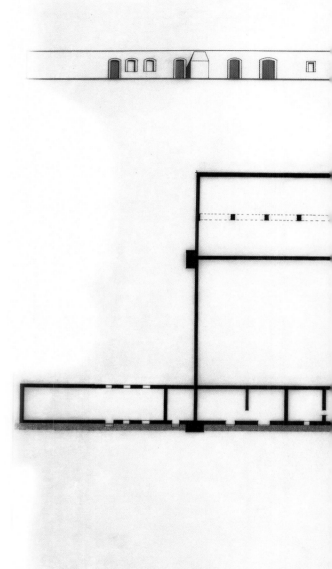

A Patio de campo   I Zaguán
B *Workers' quarters*   J *Office*
C *Granary*   K *Patio*
D *Threshing floor*   L *Dining room*
E *Cow shed*   M *Living room*
F *Corral*   N *Kitchen*
G *Chapel*   O *Orchard or garden*
H *Sacristy*

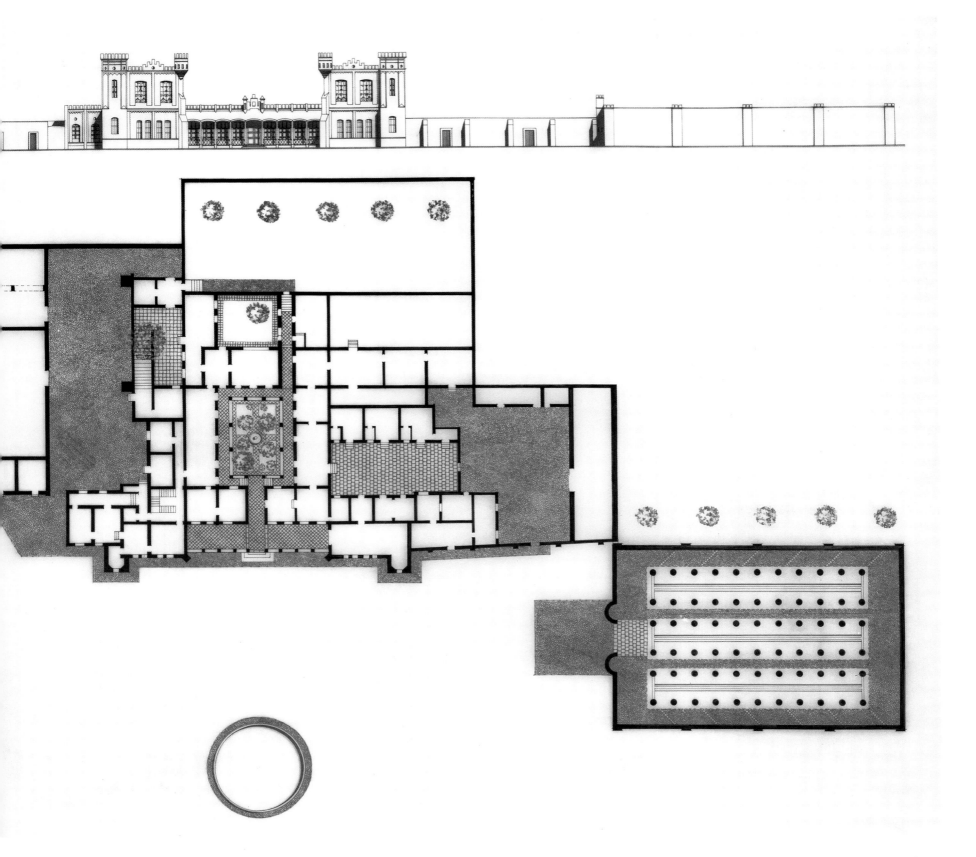

BLEDOS

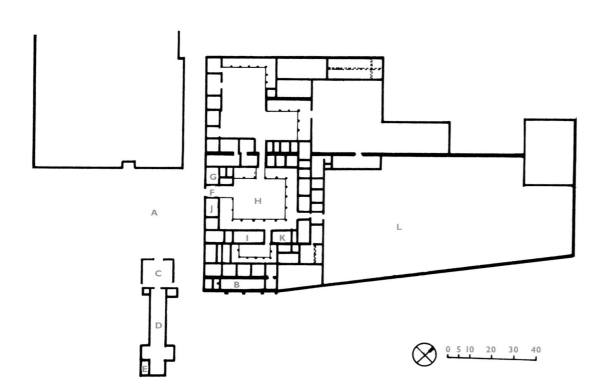

A Patio de campo   G *Office*

B *Granary*   H *Patio*

C *Atrium*   I *Dining room*

D *Chapel*   J *Living room*

E *Sacristy*   K *Kitchen*

F Zaguán   L *Orchard or garden*

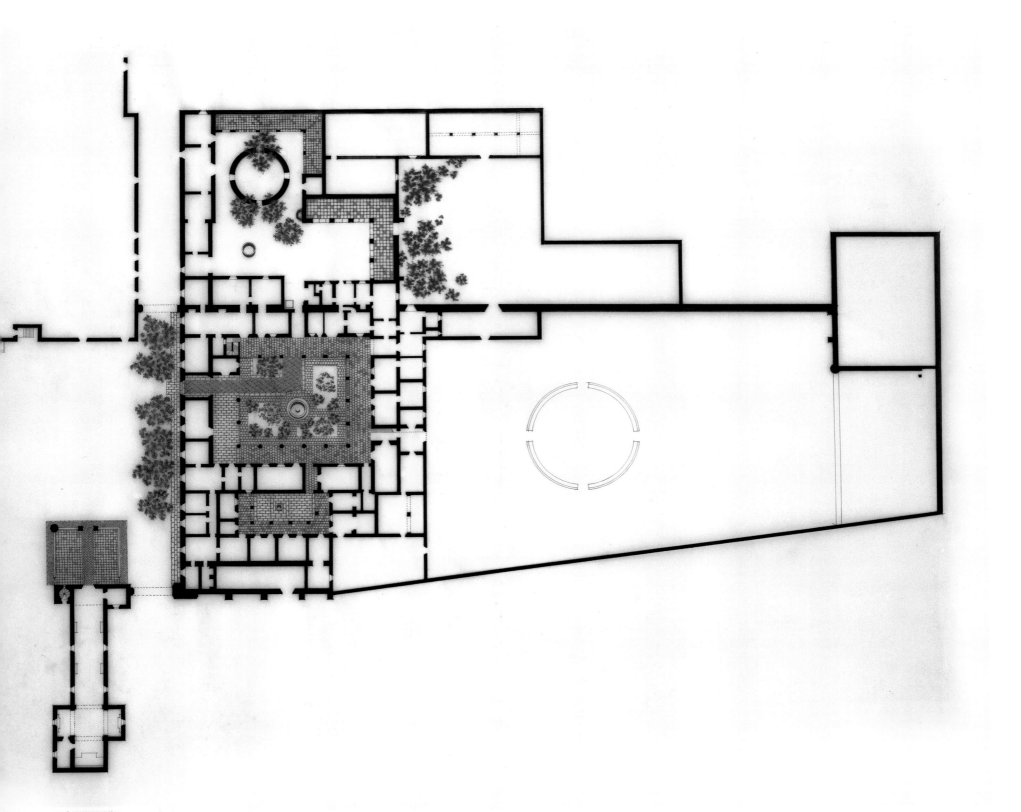

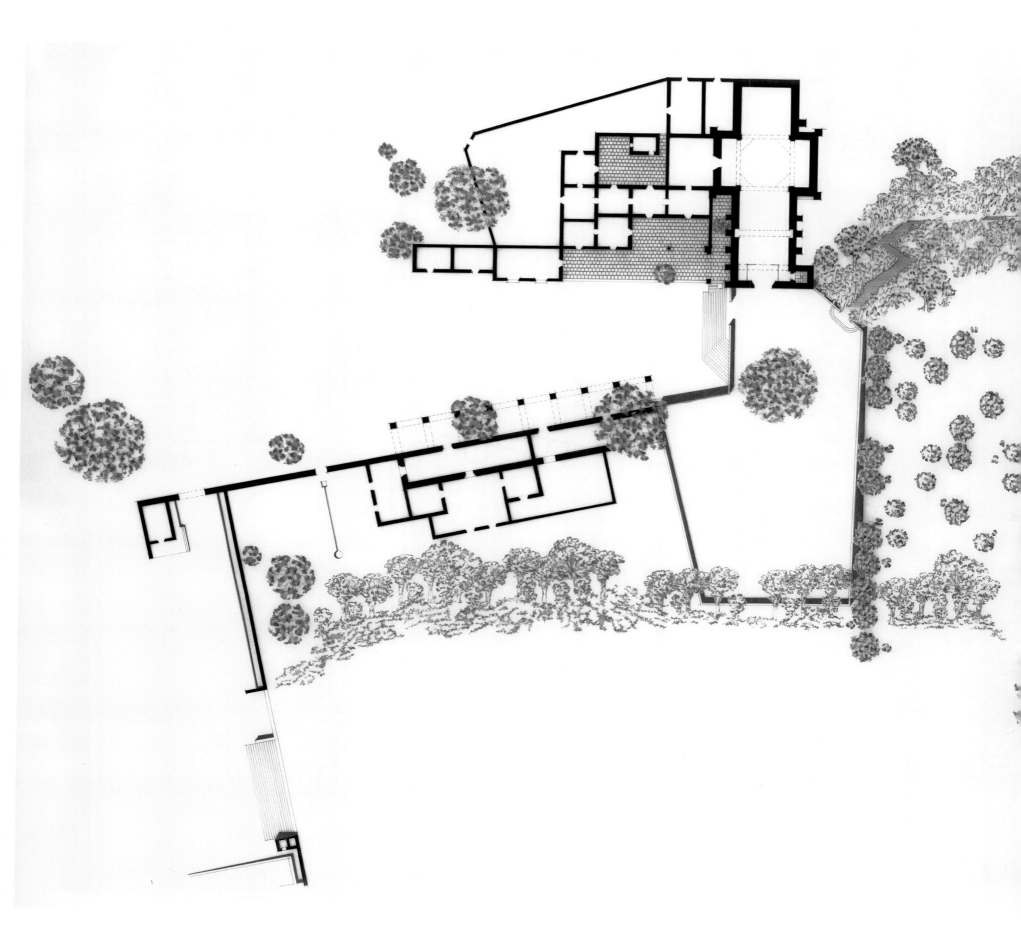

POZO DEL CARMEN—OLD HOUSE

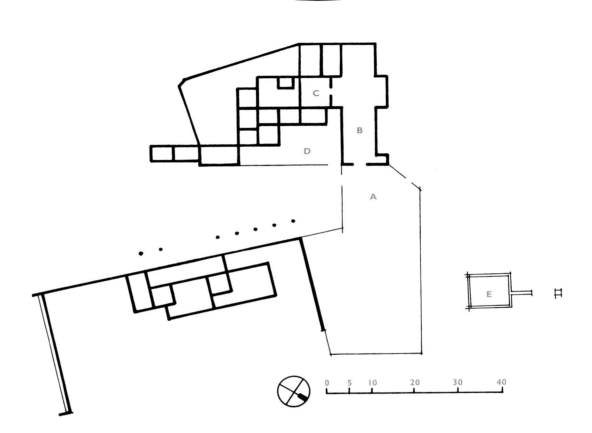

0 5 10 20 30 40

A *Atrium*
B *Chapel*
C *Sacristy*
D *Patio*
E *Well*

POZO DEL CARMEN—NEW HOUSE

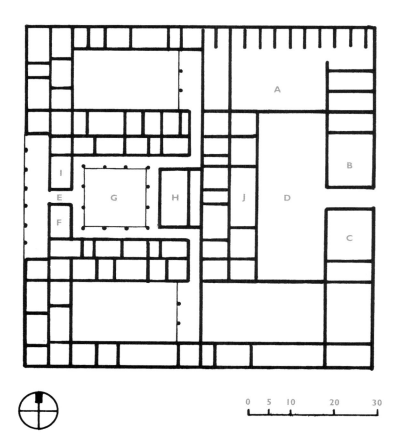

0 5 10   20   30

A Stables   F Office
B Coach house   G Patio
C Tack room   H Dining room
D Watering trough   I Living room
E Zaguán   J Kitchen

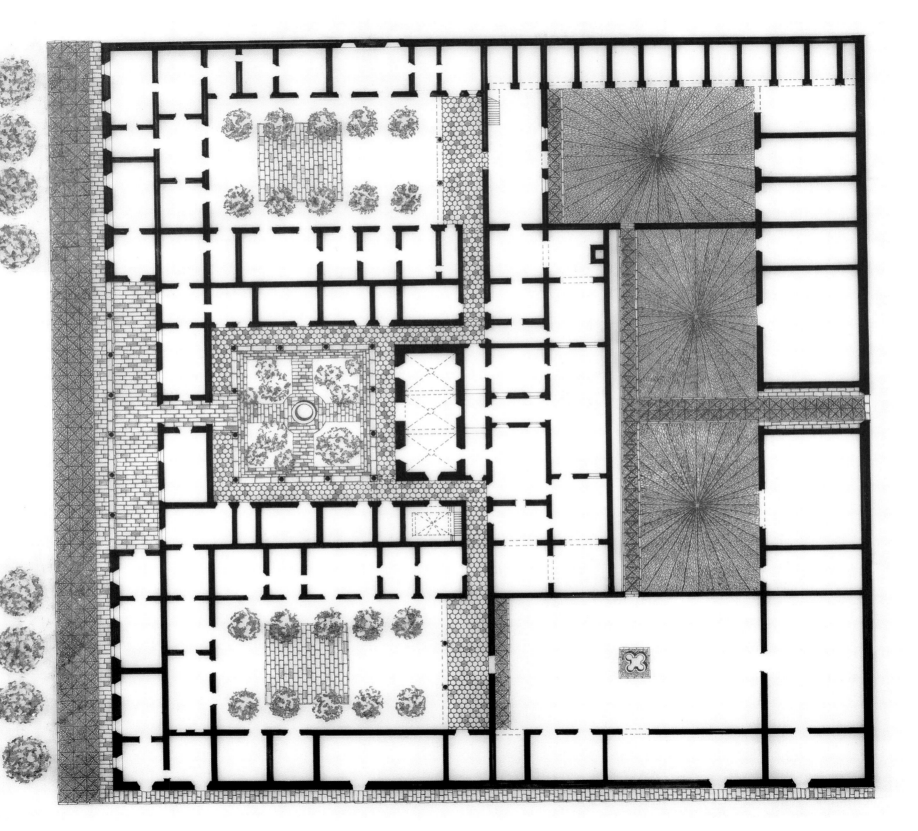

PEOTILLOS

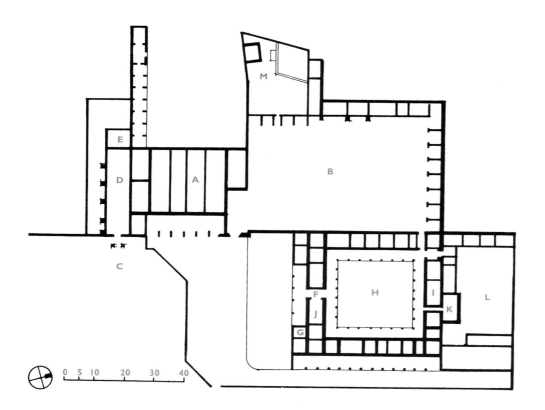

A *Granary* H *Patio*
B *Stables* I *Dining room*
C *Atrium* J *Living room*
D *Chapel* K *Kitchen*
E *Sacristy* L *Orchard or garden*
F *Zaguán* M *Well*
G *Office*

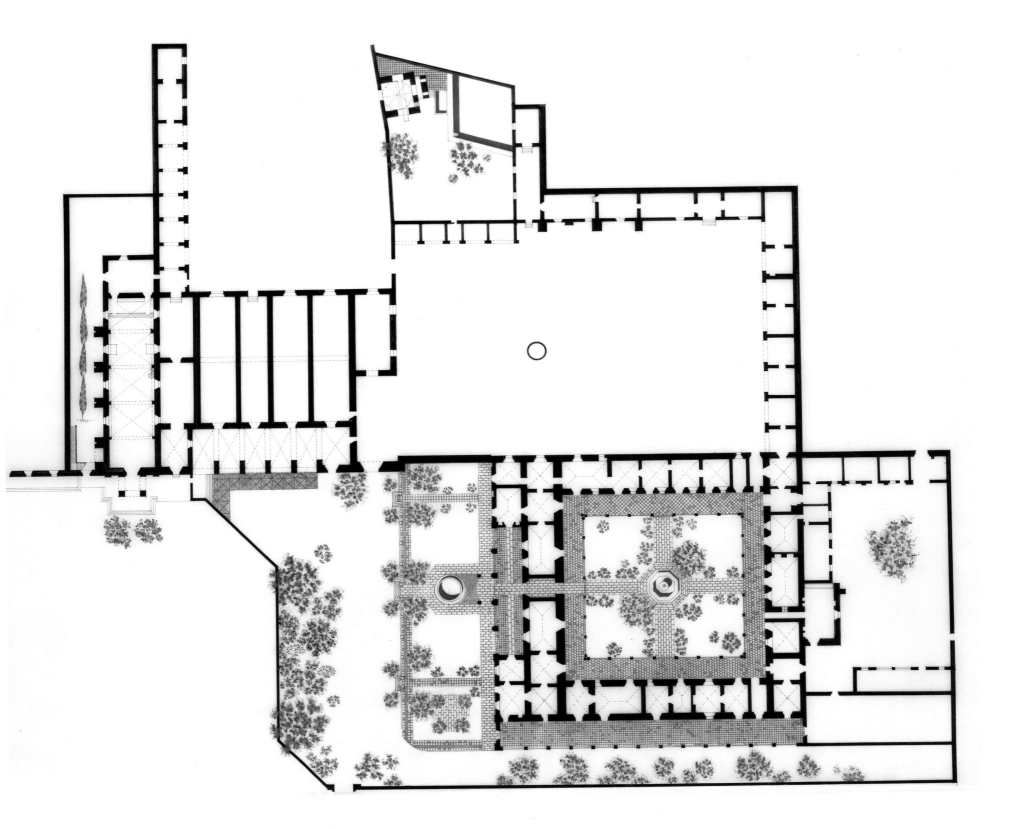

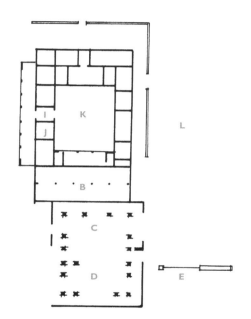

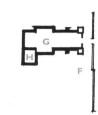

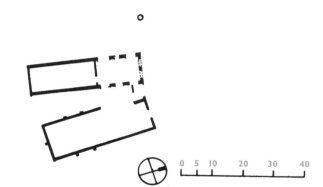

LOS REYES

0 5 10 20 30 40

A Patio de campo   G Chapel
B Granary   H Sacristy
C Stables   I Zaguán
D Corral   J Office
E Watering trough   K Patio
F Atrium   L Orchard or garden

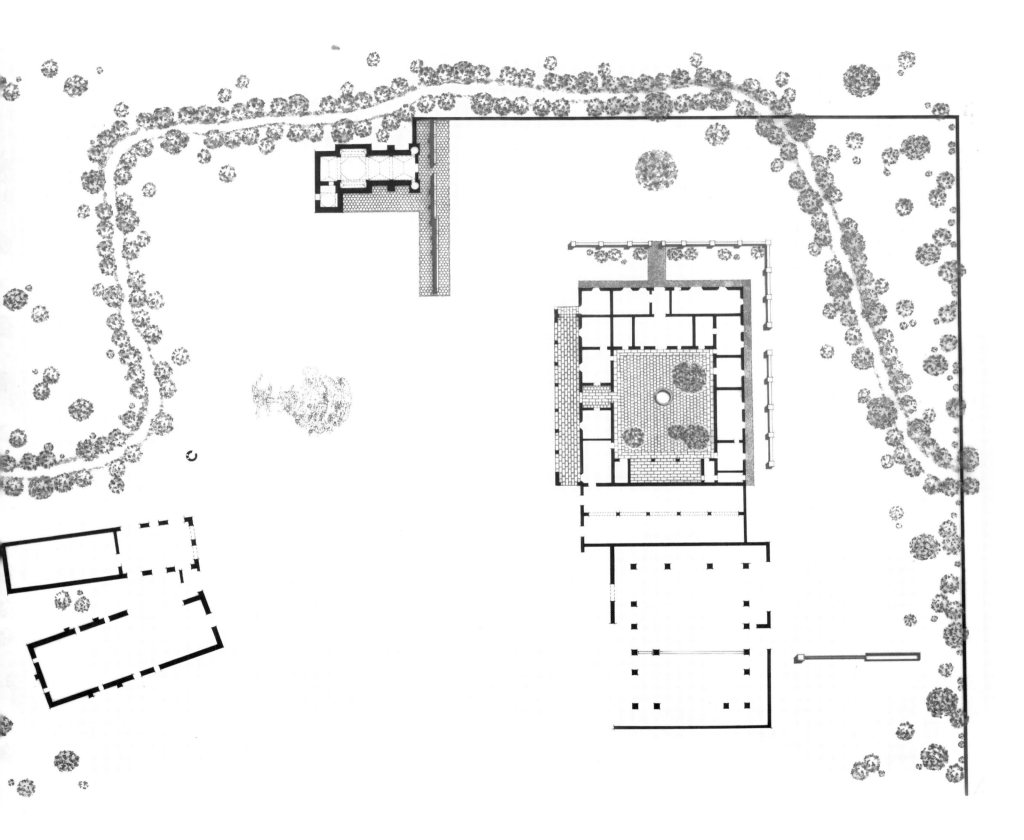

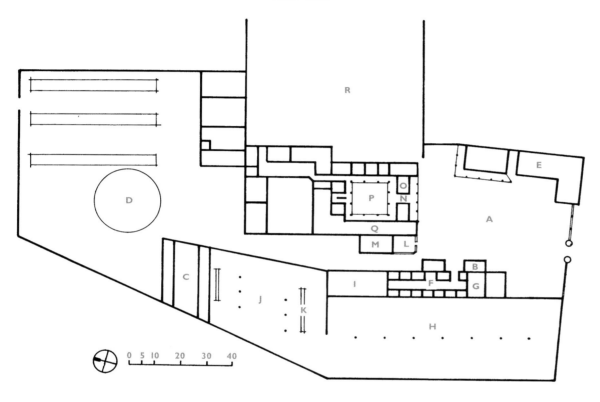

A Patio de campo	**J** *Corral*
B *Workers' quarters*	**K** *Watering trough*
C *Granary*	**L** *Atrium*
D *Threshing floor*	**M** *Chapel*
E Tinacal	**N** *Zaguán*
F *Stables*	**O** *Office*
G *Tack room*	**P** *Patio*
H *Cow shed*	**Q** *Living room*
I *Mule pen*	**R** *Orchard or garden*

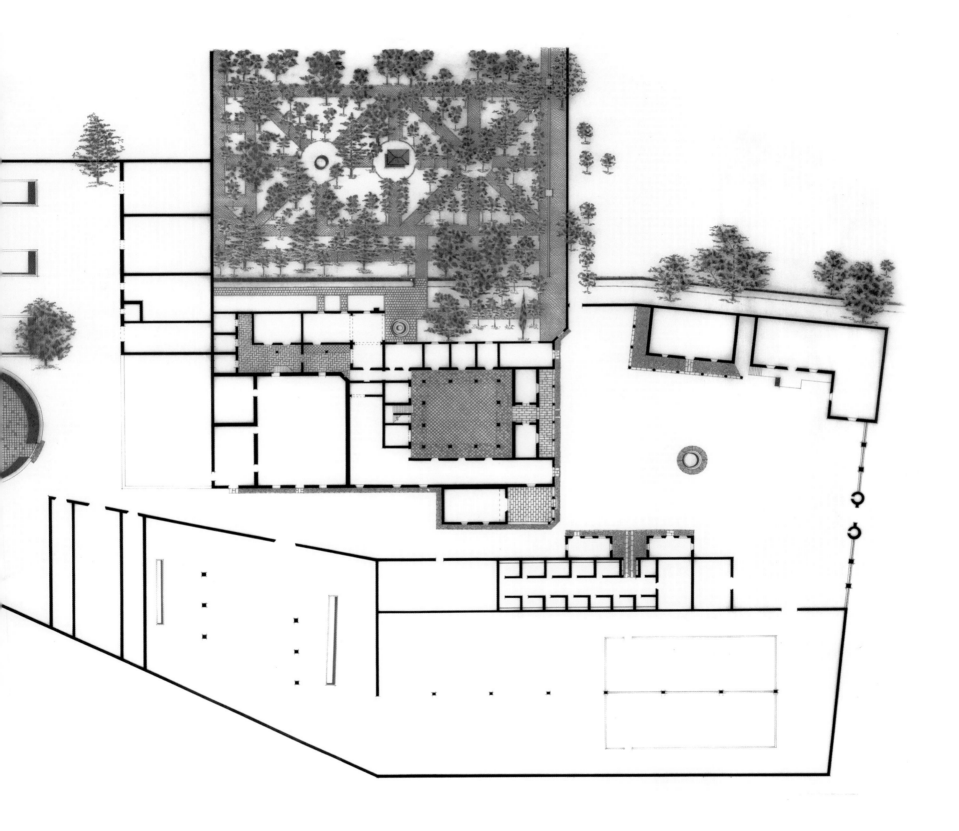

TOTOAPA

SECOND LEVEL

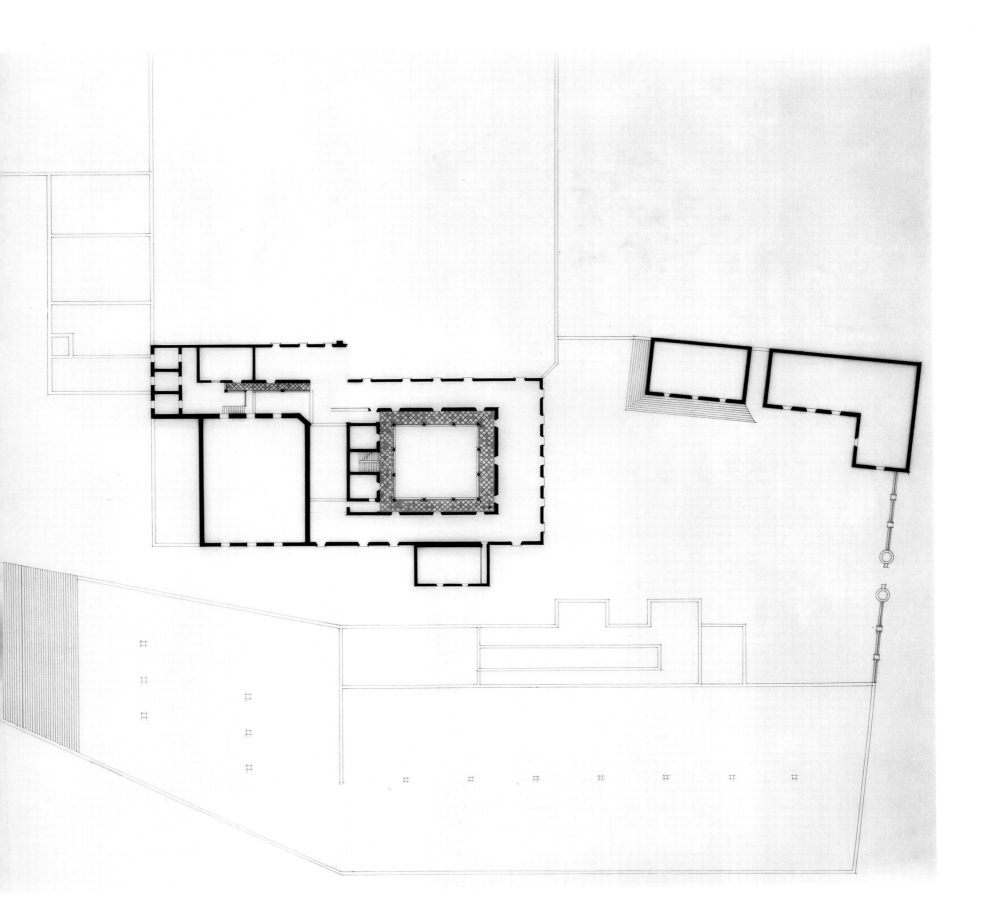

MAPS

HIDALGO

PACHUCA

TULANCINGO

APAN

1 *Arcos*	**6** *Mala Yerba*	**11** *San Joaquín*	**16** *Santa Clara*	**21** *Tepenacasco*
2 *Chimalpa*	**7** *Mal País*	**12** *San Juan Ixtilmaco*	**17** *Santa María Regla*	**22** *Tepetates*
3 *Espejel*	**8** *Montecillos*	**13** *San Lorenzo*	**18** *Santa María Tecajete*	**23** *Tetlapaya*
4 *Exquitlan*	**9** *Ocotepec*	**14** *San Miguel Regla*	**19** *Soapayuca*	**24** *Totoapa el Grande*
5 *Farías*	**10** *San Antonio Tochatlaco*	**15** *San Pedro Tochatlaco*	**20** *Tecocomulco*	**25** *Tlalayote*

26 *Venta de Cruz*		
27 *Xala*		
28 *Zontecomate*		
29 *Zotoluca*		

1 *Ameca*
2 *Cerón*
3 *Cuamantzingo*
4 *Guadalupe*
5 *Ixtafiayuca*

6 *La Compañía*
7 *La Noria*
8 *La Trinidad*
9 *Los Reyes*
10 *Mimiahuapan*

11 *Piedras Negras*
12 *Recoba*
13 *San Diego Baquedano*
14 *San Francisco Tecoac*
15 *San Francisco Soltepec*

16 *San Martín Notario*
17 *San Miguel Tepalca*
18 *San Nicolás el Grande*
19 *Santa Agueda*
20 *Santa Elena*

21 *Santa Rosa*
22 *Segura*
23 *Tecomalucan*
24 *Tenejac*
25 *Teptezala*

26 *Vista Hermosa*
27 *Xalpatlahuaya*
28 *Xonecuila*

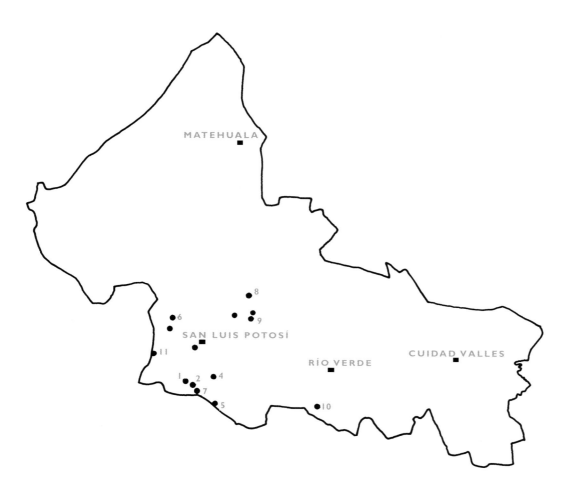

SAN LUIS POTOSÍ

MATEHUALA

SAN LUIS POTOSÍ

RÍO VERDE

CUIDAD VALLES

1 *Bledos*

2 *Carranco*

3 *Ciénega de Mata*

4 *Gogorrón*

5 *Jaral de Berrio*

6 *La Parada*

7 *La Ventilla*

8 *Peotillos*

9 *Pozo del Carmen*

10 *San Diego*

11 *Santiago*

NOTES

FOREWORD

1. The hacienda of Santa Margarita de Zontecomate in the state of Hidalgo. [Trans.]

2. Antoni Tàpies is, presumably, the twentieth-century Catalan painter. Rufino Tamayo is the internationally famous twentieth-century Mexican painter. [Trans.]

3. José María Velasco was a famous Mexican landscape painter of the mid–nineteenth century. Luis Barragán is a twentieth-century Mexican architect; Juan Rulfo, a twentieth-century Mexican writer. [Trans.]

4. Ramón López Velarde is a twentieth-century Mexican writer. [Trans.]

CHAPTER ONE

1. Chevalier, 48.
2. Ibid.
3. Ibid., 82.
4. Ibid., 97.
5. Ibid., 102.
6. Ibid., 117.

7. Ibid., 121–122.
8. Ibid., 123.
9. Florescano, 9.
10. Ibid., 9.
11. García Luna, 21.
12. Ibid., 21–22.
13. Leal and Huacuja, 99.
14. Ibid., 36.
15. Ibid., 39–40.

CHAPTER TWO

1. Fathy in Ravéreau, 12.
2. Ravéreau, 153.

CHAPTER FOUR

1. Kubler, 209.
2. García Mercadal, 64.
3. Ibid., 65.
4. Ibid.

CHAPTER SEVEN

1. Originally associated with the Moon Goddess, the manufacture of pulque has been surrounded by ritual and taboos since pre-Columbian times, and some survive to this day; for example, *tinacales* generally have an altar, and a woman's presence is forbidden. [Trans.]

CHAPTER NINE

1. This form of circular staircase, known as a *caracol* (snail), is a carryover from Roman building techniques. [Trans.]

CHAPTER TEN

1. Chueca Goitia, n.p.

2. Barragán and Rulfo are identified in the foreword to this book. Diego Rivera is a famous twentieth-century Mexican muralist. [Trans.]

GLOSSARY

Albanene. A heavy, semi-translucent, milky archival paper used by architects.

Ayuntamiento. Municipal council; same as a cabildo.

Caballería. A grant of urban land measuring 100' in width and 200' in length given to prominent citizens; a grant of farmland (the actual size of which varied from country to country) larger than a *peonía.*

Caballero. Knight, gentleman, or nobleman.

Calpulli. A clan or extended family with communally owned lands distributed for use to heads of households by the clan chieftains. The Aztecs of Tenochtitlán recognized twenty *calpulli.*

Casco. The compound of a hacienda with its numerous structures as well as its contiguous lands.

Cédula. Decree issued with royal approval.

Chacuaco. A chimney associated with boilers or kettles used in sugar production or ovens employed in the extraction of pulque and mescal.

Comal. A flat pan for cooking tortillas.

Convento. Monastery or that part of a mission of Indians where the missionaries lived and where, in some cases, the storerooms and shops were located.

Coronamiento. An adornment that tops the upper part of a building, tower, or cupola.

Encomienda. A grant made to a colonist of specified land and Indian labor. In return, the grantee, an *encomendero,* was obligated to provide for the welfare and Christian instruction of the Indians.

Espadaña. A parapet wall of a church or chapel pierced with openings or arches in which to hang bells as an alternative to a bell tower. It was in use in Spain as early as the medieval period.

Estancia. Farm or ranch.

Fanega. A dry measure approximately equal to 1.5 bushels.

Fanegada. Field necessary to sow a *fanega* of seed.

Hidalgo. Minor nobleman.

Latifundio. An exceptionally large holding of land composed of two or more haciendas.

Metate. A flat milling stone.

Open chapel. Semi-enclosed chapel built in some missions; it had an open façade facing the atria from which the priest could address a larger number of Indians than could be accommodated inside the church.

Patio de campo. Patio in that part of the compound surrounded by work areas, habitations, etc., pertaining to the laborers and production activities.

Peonía. A grant of urban land measuring 50' in width and 100' in length, or half the size of an urban *caballería,* given to ordinary individuals; a grant of farmland smaller than a *caballería,* presumably the amount of land that one peon could work in a day's time.

Pirul. A tree native to Peru.

Posa chapel. Small building incorporated into each of the four corners of the atria of some mission churches. It served as a stopping point for prayers during processionals.

Remate. An architectural element that decorates or finishes the upper part of a façade or crowns an architectural element.

Repartimiento. Initially either a small permanent Indian labor force for agricultural work or a larger seasonal one to help with harvests; later extended to mining operations.

Tabique. Fired bricks generally used for partitions or non-load-bearing walls.

Tezontle. A volcanic rock used for building in Mexico from pre-Columbian times onward.

Tinacal. Building or room containing the large vats (*tinas*) in which the juice from the pressed hearts of magueys is fermented to convert it to pulque or mescal.

Zaguán. An entry large enough to admit a carriage, or livestock in frontier areas, into a patio.

BIBLIOGRAPHY

Bazant, Jean
    1980. *Cinco haciendas mexicanas*. Mexico City:
    El Colegio de México.
Boils, Guillermo
    1982. *Las casas campesinas en el porfiriato*. Mexico
    City: Martín Casillas.
Brading, D. A.
    1978. *Haciendas and Ranchos in the Mexican Bajio*.
    Latin American Studies. Cambridge: Cambridge
    University Press.
Cabrera Ipiña de Corsi, Matilde
    1946. *Los Bledos: Memorias y leyendas de una
    hacienda*. Madrid: N.p.
Chevalier, Francois
    1981. *La formación de los latifundios en México*.
    Mexico City: Fondo de Cultura Económica.
Chueca Goitia, Fernando
    1981. *Los invariantes castizos en la arquitectura española:
    Invariantes en la arquitectura hispanoamericana*. Madrid,
    Spain: Dossat.

"Ciudad Sahagún y sus alrededores."
    1980. *Artes de México* (Mexico City) 56–57: N.p.
Dalton, Jess N.
    1945. *The Background of the Hacienda of San Miguel
    Regla*. Mexico City: N.p.
Diccionario de la Lengua Española.
    1970. Real Academia Española. Madrid: Espasa-
    Calpe.
Enciclopedia de México.
    1977. Mexico City: Enciclopedia de México.
Florescano, Enrique
    1987. "El Siglo XVII y la formación de una nueva
    oligarquía colonial." Mexico City:
    La Jornada, May 3.
García Mercadal, Fernando
    1981. *La casa popular en España*. Barcelona: Gustavo
    Gili.
García Luna, Margarita
    1981. *Haciendas porfiristas en el Edo. de México*.
    Mexico City: UNAEM.

González Sánchez, Isabel
    1969. *Haciendas y ranchos de Tlaxcala en 1712*.
    Mexico City: Instituto Nacional de Antropología
    e Historia.
Guerrero, Raúl, and Joaquín Mórtiz
    1985. *El pulque*. Mexico City: N.p.
"Haciendas de México."
    1980. *Artes de México* 79–80: N.p.
Haciendas del Siglo XIX: Haciendas coloniales.
    1986. Mexico City: Banco de Datos del Proyecto
    "Amigo."
"Las haciendas potosinas."
    1960. *Artes de México* 189: N.p.
The Haciendas of Mexico.
    1885. New York: The John C. Cocran Co.
Ibarra Grande, B. P.
    1984. *Jaral de Berrio y su marquesado*. León
    (Guanajuato), Mexico: Lumen.

Katzman, Israel
    1993. *Arquitectura mexicana del Siglo XIX.* 2d ed.
    Mexico City: Editorial Tillas.
Kubler, George
    1983. *Arquitectura mexicana del Siglo XVI.* Mexico
    City: Fondo de Cultura Económica.
Leal, Juan Felipe, and Mario Huacuja
    1982. *Economía y sistema de haciendas en México.*
    Mexico City: Era.
Libro de raya de la Hacienda de San Antonio Tula
    1870–1871. Archivo del Sr. Escandón.
Luks, Ilmar
    1980. *Tipología de la escultura decorativa hispánica en la
    arquitectura mexicana del Siglo XVIII.* Caracas:
    Centro de Investigaciones Históricas y Estéticas,
    Facultad de Arquitectura y Urbanismo,
    Universidad Central de Venezuela.
Meade, Mercedes
    1984. *San Bartolomé del Monte.* Tlaxcala: Talleres
    Gráficos de Tlaxcala.
Paniagua, José Ramón
    1980. *Vocabulario básico de arquitectura.* Madrid:
    Ediciones Cátedra.
Ravéreau, André
    1981. *Le M'Zab: Une Leçon d'Architecture.* Preface by
    Hassan Fathy. Paris: Editions Sindbad.

Romero de Terreros y Vinnet
    1956. *Antiguas haciendas.* Mexico City: Patria.
Shneider, Pierre, Michel Saudan, and Silvia Saudan-
    Skira
    1985. *De la Villa en Venetie.* Geneva: Atelier d'Edition
    "Le Septieme Rou."
Tovar de Teresa, Guillermo
    1981. *México barroco.* Mexico City: S.A.H.O.P.
Toussaint, Manuel
    1983. *Arte colonial en México.* Mexico City:
    Universidad Nacional Autónoma de México.
Unamuno, Miguel de
    1979. *En torno al casticismo.* Madrid: Espasa-Calpe.
Vargas-Lobsinger, María
    1984. *La Hacienda de "La Concha": Una empresa
    algodonera de La Laguna.* Mexico City: Universidad
    Nacional Autónoma de México.
Vivienda campesina en México.
    1978. Mexico City: S.A.H.O.P.
Womack, John, Jr.
    1983. *Zapata y la Revolución Mexicana.* Mexico City:
    S.E.P.